"*To Construct Peace* deals with peacemaking in a fresh and compelling way. Michael True's very special gift is to convey in brief narratives the creative and energizing stories of peacemakers, peace communities, and peace movements....His narratives are constantly lit up by golden nuggets of citations from his wide reading."

Eileen Egan
Author, *Such a Vision of the Street: Mother Teresa*
A Founder of Pax Christi

"This collection by Michael True is a truly fascinating collection of vignettes about courageous people who seek peace and justice—often in unconventional ways. The stories are told deftly and incisively. We learn intriguing things about Penny Lernoux, Archbishop Hunthausen, Noam Chomsky, and over two dozen other seekers of peace.

"*To Construct Peace* is destined to be as popular as the same author's 1985 *Justice Seekers, Peace Makers*, now in its fourth printing.

"We yearn today for saints. We hunger for the martyrology. This welcome volume will help satisfy those aspirations the Holy Spirit placed in us. Michael True is a superb storyteller. He continues to inspire us with his compelling chapters about heroic persons whom we admire, envy, and seek to imitate."

Robert F. Drinan, S.J.
Professor, Georgetown University Law Center

"Michael True wrote *To Construct Peace* to lift the cloud of historical anonymity that envelopes so many peacemakers. In thirty short essays True highlights some of these 'resourceful, courageous' people. The thirty individuals and groups in *To Construct Peace* are wonderfully diverse. The one thing they have in common is a deep commitment to peace-making. This is one of this book's special contributions: it demonstrates how nearly universal the call to be peacemakers is. I recommend it highly."

Walter F. Sullivan
Bishop of Richmond
Bishop President of Pax Christi, USA

"This log of rather ordinary heroes is a testimony to courage, commitment, and compassion. Each story taken separately is moving, but bound together. Michael True's profiles swell into a tidal wave of nonviolent action for social change. These stories need to be told over and over, until their lives become the model for our own."

Anne McCarthy, O.S.B.
National Coordinator
Pax Christi USA

"Michael True's pocket-sized portraits of peacemakers around the world are sure to catch the fancy of anyone interested in the cause of peace through justice. The best way to teach peace is by presenting the personal example of real people who see the need to do something about it. The peacemakers in this book come from widely different backgrounds. Some are sung, some unsung, but all are heros in their own way.

"*To Construct Peace* will inspire the hesitating and affirm the committed. Peace is worth what it takes to construct it."

Gerard A. Vanderhaar
Professor of Religion and Peace Studies
Author, *Active Nonviolence: A Way of Personal Peace*

"Everyone involved or even interested in the encouraging spread of peace studies courses and programs in high schools and in colleges will welcome True's second 'sampler' of individuals and groups who have made special contributions to peace and social justice. The brevity of the summaries should stir readers' appetites for more detail, and True's bibliographical guides will lead them to sources that will satisfy that hunger."

Gordon C. Zahn
Professor Emeritus in Sociology
University of Massachusetts

"To read *To Construct Peace* by Michael True is to be struck with hope. Capsulized lives of peacemaking individuals and movements draw you into that River of Hope that runs just underneath what often seems to be a Life of Desperation.

"This work will be especially useful as spiritual reading, reading that nurtures your spirit and inspires you to 'keep going on.' Here are the heroes and heroic movements that we especially need at this time. These are the 'saints' that really matter to us, the people who will really get us closer to God.

"The select bibliographies are quite welcome, especially for school purposes."

Dr. Joseph Torma
Director, Institute for Justice and Peace
Walsh College

"*To Construct Peace* brings to a general audience the results of careful research into neglected corners of the human story, and especially of the American story. Here is history of peace and justice that is at once scholarly and engaging. This book is good news for anyone who still thinks that history is all about wars."

Mary Evelyn Jegen, S.N.D.
Staff, Pax Christi International

"Michael True keeps alive knowledge of women and men—most individuals, a few communities—bound together by their willingness to go beyond the criticism of war and violence to construct peace. In True's brief essays, authentic prophets find renewed voice, to the benefit of us all."

David J. O'Brien
Loyola Professor of Roman Catholic Studies
College of the Holy Cross

"In his *To Construct Peace*, Michael True has assembled an inspiring collection of architects for peace. This book, like his previous *Justice Seekers, Peace Makers*, presents a variety of prophets who have struggled and suffered for the cause of peace. The title is very appropriate since, as True shows, peace is the result of a patient, piece by piece, day by day, building in every part of the globe. In True's mind, peace is a universal call.

"The approach of the author is equally varied. It encompasses peace music of Joan Baez, political struggles of the young Stephen Biko, courageous reporting of Penny Lernoux, and peace confrontations of the Chinese youth in Tien An Men Square. In a gripping way the author speaks of the peaceful, nonviolent witnessing of our contemporary martyrs in El Salvador, as well as of the loving labors of the indomitable Dorothy Day.

"*To Construct Peace* is a compelling invitation to the reader to recommit oneself to the gospel challenge of peace: 'Let each one seek peace and pursue it.'"

Mary A. Dooley, S.S.J.
President
College of Our Lady of the Elms

TO CONSTRUCT PEACE

30 More
Justice Seekers,
Peace Makers

MICHAEL TRUE

TWENTY-THIRD PUBLICATIONS

Mystic, Connecticut 06355

Twenty-Third Publications
185 Willow Street
P.O. Box 180
Mystic CT 06355
(203) 536-2611
800-321-0411

ISBN 0-89622-487-2
Library of Congress Catalog Card Number 91-65199

DEDICATION

To
Herb and Betty Ann True
Bob and Sue True

ACKNOWLEDGMENTS

Many friends and associates helped with information about the people and communities in this book. Jane Morrissey, S.S.J., generously offered materials about the life and work of her friend, the late Penny Lernoux; Kathy Knight shared memories of her close friend and co-worker, the late Maura Clarke, M.M.; Elizabeth Ann True, Fitchburg State College Library, provided important materials, including lyrics to Peter Gabriel's "Biko"; William Stafford kindly lent the remarkable photograph of himself as a young C.O.; Ed Spivey, Jr., art director of Sojourners, provided the photos of Penny Lernoux and Michael Harrington; and Jo Roberts of The Catholic Worker provided that publication's logo. For such contributions, each of these persons—and particularly Roger Trahan—deserves a special thank you.

In addition to sources cited at the end of each chapter, I am grateful to my editor, Helen Coleman, as well as to Priscilla Berthiaume, Reference Librarian, Assumption College; Philip Runkel, Catholic Worker Archives, Marquette University. Michael O'Shea, Faculty Development Committee, and Richard Oehling, Assumption College, listened and responded to requests for assistance on projects leading to this book. Philippe Poisson, librarian, has been the kind of friend and colleague that one can only acknowledge, though never truly repay.

I appreciate, also, editorial suggestions by George Aubin, Anne Monica True, and—always and especially—Mary Patricia Delaney True. Recognizing their assistance, I must add that these people bear no responsibility for any errors. The dedication to my brothers and sisters-in-law is a small acknowledgment of their encouragement and generosity over the years.

CONTENTS

TO CONSTRUCT PEACE

INTRODUCTION

"To Construct Peace" is a phrase from Muriel Rukeyser's "Poem," about "men and women/ Brave, setting up signals across vast distances,/ Considering a nameless way of living, of almost unimagined values." Thinking of such people, the poet says, reflectively,

> We would try to imagine them...
> To construct peace, to make love, to reconcile
> Waking with sleeping, ourselves with each other,
> Ourselves with ourselves.

It's a large order. Yet in the past and even in this violent century, men and women in every culture have worked to reconcile their differences nonviolently and "to create the beloved community," as Martin Luther King suggested. In the face of considerable opposition, they remained faithful to these personal and social values, and enriched our lives by doing so.

The purpose of these brief essays in biographical-history is two-fold: (1) to suggest the diversity and vitality of that peace community and the cultural tradition that sustains it; and (2) to outline the "geography" of that tradition, particularly in the U.S., and in a few other countries as well.

"All it takes for violence to flourish," to paraphrase Edmund Burke, "is for a few good persons to do nothing." For although violence in tribal societies may be primarily ritualistic, in modern societies it becomes a rational decision, coolly thought out. Powerful political, military, or religious people, with well-defined interests, launch wars. Then ordinary people tolerate them "despite their suicidal quality and the suffering, oppression and absurdity involved," as anthropological psychiatrist Bernard Huyghe has argued.

In a world—or an imperial country—that spends more money, talent, and resources on armaments than on human services, many of us do nothing until the consequences of these priorities—war and hunger—pile up on our doorsteps. Only then do we look for new ways of doing things and setting new priorities to alleviate the suffering. If we are lucky, traditions in our own families and communities suggest ways to "make love, not war."

Throughout history, resourceful, courageous people have come up with ways of "making peace" in the midst of violence and injustice. Some are well known—Gandhi, Dorothy Day, Martin Luther King, for example; but many are forgotten, ignored, or neglected. Too busy or modest to call attention to themselves, they are often lost to history, including those who, in recording it, prefer to write about "making war."

The brief portraits that follow describe the lives of individuals and small communities who worked for the common good. Acting alone or in association with others, they "kept on keepin' on," as Etheridge Knight used to say, so that from the pages of history, their patience and persistence shine forth.

None of the individuals who committed themselves "to construct peace" is a saint in the conventional, pretty-as-a-picture sense. Each of them is all too human—flawed, inconsistent (like the rest of us)—as spouses, children, closest friends, and biographers sometimes attest. Several of them died as martyrs to a cause; others worked (or continue to work) modestly, day after day, to build a civic culture that a fragile humanity depends upon for survival. Finding themselves engaged in elemental struggles against oppression in some little corner of the world, they surprised themselves most of all. As Dorothy Day, a major influence on the American tradition of nonviolence, said of her own resistance to the air-raid drills in New York City in the 1950s, "I got pushed into it"—in her case by Ammon Hennacy and Karl Meyer.

Several of these peacemakers got "pushed into" standing in a picket line or risking arrest for civil disobedience, in a way that significantly influenced their lives and writings. Others, especially those who wound up in jail, were radicalized by that experience. Might the world be a better place if more of us faced similar tests, took similar risks, for justice's sake? Perhaps.

As a group, the men and women discussed in the following chapters represent a wide variety of talents, backgrounds, nationalities, and dispositions: clergy and laity, activists and artists, war veterans and pacifists, workers and scholars, young students and grandparents. Although U.S. citizens dominate the list, several are native to or permanent residents of El Salvador, India, Austria, England, Brazil, South Africa, and China.

The book's emphasis upon diversity has to do with another central truth about peacemaking. In order to alter the present priorities, we need to build as large a community of people making peace as we now tolerate making war. Standing at the bottom of a ramp in the Pentagon one summer afternoon, I was stunned at the sight of that thundering herd tumbling out of Department of Defense offices at quitting time: engineers, computer programmers, janitors, secretaries, researchers, many in army, navy, and marine uniforms (mainly colonels and above). Although I knew the dollar-value of the annual Pentagon budget, I had, until then, no immediate sense of what the payroll for war-making meant in brain-and-people power.

To repeat: The only way of dissipating the violent consequences of a huge, hard-working, talented group of war-makers is to build a larger, harder-working community of peace-makers. (At times, that will simply mean the same people working for different goals, a change that many of them might welcome.) Kenneth Boulding has said that the world's troubles, including war, result not so much from "a lack of good will, as a lack of knowledge as to how to make good will effective." In a very real sense, he and others in these pages offer practical ways of doing just that.

In addition to biographical facts, I have included a few quotations—from letters, essays, poems, interviews—where people say how they came to their vocation as peacemakers. Usually, it happened in a round-about way, as events brought them to a particular place at a particular time. By remaining faithful to humane values, they followed their (often) natural inclination to make the world a better place. In doing so, they offer choices—"signals," as the Rukeyser poem says—about how we might conduct ourselves in similar situations.

Every culture, every region of the world has its own history of nonviolent activists, persons who refused to tolerate humiliation, violence, or oppression. That history includes thousands of citizens, young and old, famous or relatively unknown, who commit themselves to and involve others in the herculean task of ending injustice and constructing peace. In acknowledging their work for the common good, I hope also to challenge the reader (and the author) to "carry it on."

A final note on the order of presentation: The portraits, people, and communities are arranged in chronological, though reverse, order—that is, with contemporary figures first, then moving back in history through the early 20th and 19th centuries. Although this book resembles my earlier one, I have made an effort to avoid duplicating information included in its predecessor, *Justice Seekers, Peace Makers* (Mystic, Conn.: Twenty-Third Publications, 1985), a kind of a companion volume. I am aware at the same time that my choices are sometimes representative—or arbitrary, if you will. Choosing one person, I sometimes omit someone equally famous or remarkable, someone who has contributed admirably to justice and peace. In choosing a journalist, I decided on Penny Lernoux, though several others—I. F. Stone, Nat Hentoff, Colman McCarthy—belong in a book of this kind as well. Similarly, among activists, I chose David Dellinger rather than Glenn Smiley, Jim Peck, Bayard Rustin, Marj Swann, Barbara Deming, Bernard Lafayette, who also occupy important places in the history of nonviolent social change. Each country, indeed each region of this country, has its heroes and heroines who deserve mention in a similar book of portraits; it awaits another author.

The list of references at the end of each portrait refers to writings and artifacts by and about the subject. In each case, I try to mention references that are easily accessible in school and public libraries or through well-known justice and peace organizations throughout the U.S.

Young Catholic Workers

CATHOLIC WORKER

THE ORIGINS ARE POSITIVELY BIBLICAL: A MUSTARD SEED fell on rocky soil at Union Square, near 14th Street and Broadway, in New York City. For six decades, it grew and grew into a deeply-rooted, sheltering tree—today an arboretum.

In Spokane, Colorado Springs, Davenport, Rock Hill, and Worcester, as well as in Los Angeles, St. Louis, Chicago, Baltimore, and New York, and in the Netherlands and Australia, street people find food, clothing, and shelter in soup kitchens maintained by young Catholic Workers. Since 1933, when its members first distributed 2,500 copies of the *Catholic Worker* newspaper in Lower Manhattan, the Catholic Worker movement has provided hospitality for hundreds of thousands of men and women whom nobody else cared about.

Initiated by Peter Maurin (1879-1949), an itinerate teacher and worker, and Dorothy Day (1897-1980), a journalist, shortly after their first meeting in December 1932, the movement has drawn three generations of talented workers and organizers, writers and artists, into its network. In the process, it has remained a significant influence on American Catholicism, as well as on the social, intellectual, and literary history of the U.S.

By her life and writings, Dorothy Day is surely the most visible and influential figure in the movement. But she regarded Peter Maurin as her teacher; because of them, thousands of "ordinary people" have helped to initiate houses, farms, newspapers, and campaigns for nonviolent social change for over six decades. Some spent a brief period with the Worker—among them Michael Harrington, John Cogley, Ade Bethune, J. F. Powers, William Everson, John Cort, Jim Forest, Charlie King; others have spent much of their lives—Ammon Hennacy, Karl Meyer, Frank Donovan, Rita Corbin, Brendan and Willa Walsh, Tom and Monica Cornell. Workers include scores of priests, nuns, and laity, many of them well-known in various professions and walks of life. Because of their admiration for Dorothy Day, their contributions to the movement, or their writings about her, many others have regarded themselves as "fellow travelers" of the movement. These include Gordon Zahn, Robert Coles, William Miller, David O'Brien, and Robert Ellsberg, not to mention the late W. H. Auden, Thomas Merton, and Fritz Eichenberg.

Visiting the hundred or more houses across the U.S., one inevitably meets young men and women, many of them students, for whom the Catholic Worker has been a kind of "agronomic university," as Peter Maurin hoped it would be. There, they learn much about "the whole rotten system," as Dorothy Day used to say, and meet the victims of violence and injustice for the first time. There young people learn how to become "part of the solution" rather than remain "part of the problem." Many go on to extend "the beloved community" through their own efforts, as they live lives of voluntary poverty among the poor or follow a more conventional pattern of marriage, family, and profession. Whatever they choose to do, their lives carry the mark of days, months, or years actively involved with the Catholic Worker, and through them the movement continues to flourish into the third generation. Daily, across the U.S., young Catholic Workers feed the hungry, house the homeless, set up food pantries and medical treatment centers, comfort the sick, bury the dead, periodically going to trial or into jail for resisting capital punishment, the arms race, and other injustices.

Each day it keeps going seems, to an outsider, a kind of miracle, as some give their lives for these values; others have their houses closed down for failing to meet a local building code. On worse days, they stand among the ashes, after a thoughtless guest falls asleep, maybe drunk, with a cigarette in his or her mouth. In June 1991, Matt Devenney of the Community Stewpot, in Jackson, Mississippi, was actually gunned down by a regular patron with a history of mental illness; Devenney, a 33-year-old husband and father, had directed the Stewpot for several years. Frequently, young workers simply burn out, after years of sharing the daily rough and tumble of the inner city poor and the endless stream of "undeserving poor," as Bernard Shaw called them, that line up for soup and hospitality and whatever else is freely offered.

Around these Catholic Workers, other life-giving communities form, some agitating for farm workers' or women's rights, environmental protection or credit unions, land trusts, peace fellowships, draft and war tax resistance. How lucky any town or city is that harbors a Catholic Worker house, for the unaccounted and often unacknowledged blessings it brings in helping to preserve community in urban settings otherwise rife with violence, hunger, poverty, and neglect.

Each Catholic Worker house, in varying degrees, is a kind of oasis in which these values are made visible and concrete. And after sixty years, a small library of fiction, poetry, plays, artwork, films, and nonfiction tells the story again and again, so that no child growing up and surely no person associated with Christianity should remain ignorant of its powerful example.

Dorothy Day, a born storyteller, understood the power of narrative as the instrument of "spreading the word," and she told the Catholic Worker story over and over again, especially in *The Long*

Loneliness (1952), the story of her conversion, and *The Loaves and Fishes* (1963), and continually in a paragraph or two in her monthly column, "On Pilgrimage." So did Ammon Hennacy in *The Book of Ammon* (1954, 1970) and Robert Ellsberg, in his introduction to *Little by Little: The Selected Writings of Dorothy Day* (1983).

At the end of *The Long Loneliness,* Dorothy Day wrote that "We have all known the long loneliness and we have learned that the only solution is love and that love comes with community. It all happened while we sat there talking, and it is still going on." Forty years after she wrote that memorable sentence, it's *still* going on, in evenings of clarification of thought at houses across the U.S., at Ammon Hennacy House in Los Angeles and at the Dorothy Day Soup Kitchen in Rock Hill, South Carolina, in the pages of the *Catholic Worker* and *The Catholic Radical.*

There are many models for the Catholic Worker and many routes to it. Some Houses serve twelve people one meal a week; some serve six hundred people three meals a day. Some Houses take in anyone without a place to sleep. Some distribute free food from a continually replenished pantry, while others house people visiting relatives at state or federal prisons.

Some Workers devote their lives to the movement; others stay for awhile, then move on to other commitments. Scott and Claire Schaeffer-Duffy, for example, met shortly after they graduated from Holy Cross College and the University of Virginia, Charlottesville, respectively and set up houses for men and women in a rough, poor neighborhood in Washington, D.C. After their marriage, they moved to Worcester, Massachusetts, where they established the House of SS. Francis and Therese, and where they live with their three children and various guests, publish a handsome, informative monthly, *The Catholic Radical,* and go to trial and to jail for civil disobedience at the GTE plant nearby, which makes the brains of the MX missile; at Electric Boat, Groton, Connecticut, which manufactures and launches nuclear submarines; or at Westover, Massachusetts, Airforce Base, from which bombers flew to Vietnam and troops went to the Persian Gulf. The Schaeffer-Duffys also teach religious education to children in a local parish, run a summer peace camp for children, and sell bran muffins and wheat bread to raise money for all the projects.

At Viva House Catholic Worker, Willa and Brendan Walsh live with their daughter, Kate, in Baltimore's inner city, where they feed thirty people three times a week and provide hospitality and health care for a community of needy people. On the walls of the soup kitchen and dining room, Willa's silk screens tell part of the story of their commitment to nonviolent social change. The Walshs had moved to the city and married several years before they supported the Catonsville Nine (Philip Berrigan, the Melvilles, and others) who burned draft files in an effort to end the Vietnam war.

Similarly, Brian Terrell and Betsy Keenan married, after working together at St. Joseph's House in Lower Manhattan and the Catholic Worker Farm in Tivoli, New York. After seven years at Peter Maurin House, Davenport, Iowa, they now homestead four acres of land, sell rag rugs and small crafts in Maloy, Iowa, 100 miles southwest of Des Moines.

In Hawaii, on that state's "big island," Jim Albertini and his wife oversee a Catholic Worker farm and retreat center. He too spent time in jail, for "swimming in" to protest nuclear weapons in and around Pearl Harbor. And in Rock Hill, South Carolina, a community of parents and grade school children, with encouragement from David Valtierra, Congregation of the Oratory, initiated a Dorothy Day Soup Kitchen.

Just off Second Avenue, and around the corner from the best Ukrainian restaurant in New York City, Jane Sammon and Cassey Temple oversee the many activities of the Catholic Worker's "national office." They edit the monthly *Catholic Worker*, still a penny a copy, as it was in the 1930s, with informative articles on the Philippines, for example, or tax resistance, with letters from houses and communities around the world, and announcements of Friday Evening "Clarifications of Thought," including poetry readings or urgent messages from young activists and scholars. At the New York houses, as well as at the Marquette University archives in Milwaukee, journalists and historians, young students and seasoned scholars phone or drop by for news and information to include in new anthologies of writings or portraits (like this one) of Catholic Workers, young and old, active or deceased.

Thus do Houses of Hospitality, "agronomic universities," and other Catholic Worker communities continue to flourish, much as

Peter Maurin envisioned them decades ago. First he, then Ammon Hennacy, pushed Dorothy Day along a pilgrimage that she followed and chartered for so many others, including the talented, resourceful, and courageous young men and women who carry it on.

BY YOUNG CATHOLIC WORKERS
By Little and By Little: Selected Writings of Dorothy Day. Robert Ellsberg, ed. New York: Alfred A. Knopf, 1983.

Cook, Jack. *Rags of Time: A Season in Prison.* Boston: Beacon Press, 1972.

A Revolution of the Heart: Essays on the Catholic Worker. Patrick G. Coy, ed. Philadelphia: Temple University Press, 1988.

Ellis, Mark H. *A Year at the Catholic Worker.* New York: Paulist Press, 1978.

ABOUT YOUNG CATHOLIC WORKERS
Coles, Robert, and Jon Erikson. *A Spectacle Unto the World: The Catholic Worker Movement.* New York: Viking Press, 1973.

Miller, William D. *A Harsh and Dreadful Love: Dorothy Day and the Catholic Worker Movement.* New York: Liveright, 1973.

Piehl, Mel. *Breaking Bread: The Catholic Worker and the Origin of Catholic Radicalism in America.* Philadelphia: Temple University Press, 1982.

Stephen Biko

1946-1977

You can blow out a candle
But you can't blow out a fire
Once the flame begins to catch
The wind will blow it higher
Oh Biko, Biko, because Biko...
The eyes of the world are
watching now...

HE WAS "QUITE SIMPLY THE GREATEST MAN I HAVE EVER had the privilege to know," according to a writer who met and interviewed many world leaders. In saying this, Donald Woods meant that Stephen Biko "had the most impressive array of qualities and abilities in that sphere of life which determines the fates of most people—politics."

For a man who died when he was only thirty and never traveled outside his own country, Stephen Biko had a remarkable following; as the editors of *Christianity and Crisis* said at the time of his death, his face and mind were known across the world. Years later, he still occupies a special place among people struggling for human rights—in history and literature, in film (especially the award-winning *Cry, Freedom*) and song (Peter Gabriel's "Biko," quoted above).

Biko became famous as a leader in the struggle to end apartheid and to build a democratic society in South Africa. In death, he joined thousands of black people who, like him, had been victimized by white settlers since foreign settlements in the mid-17th century. Often torn by tribal conflicts and interracial battles, Africans had neither guns nor horses to face the superior technology of white invaders until the end of the 18th century.

Over three centuries, many white people died also in conflicts between white Afrikaners—descendants of early Dutch, German, and Huguenot settlers—and later British settlers. As the twentieth century began, these two groups fought one another in the Boer War. Shortly afterward, Mohandas Gandhi led an important movement resisting discrimination against Indians, before he returned to his native country and helped to end British rule. Among the black leaders in recent history, Albert Luthuli, winner of the Nobel Prize for Peace, and Nelson Mandela, now released from prison, are particularly well-known; among many terrible incidents, the Sharpeville Massacre (1960), in which South African forces killed 70 Africans and wounded 186 others, evoked the strongest protest from people around the world.

Since 1948, the Nationalist Party has been the party in power, dominated by Afrikaners, who make up 60 percent of the white population in South Africa. In its efforts to perpetuate rule by a white minority, in a country in which eighty percent of the people are black, the Nationalists implemented a number of repressive measures; systematically carried out, these apartheid policies confined blacks to particular regions of the country and denied them basic human rights. Of several major black leaders associated with this terrible period, Stephen Biko was the first to die. It happened in this way. In 1961, in an effort to crush two popular black movements, the Nationalist party banned Nelson Mandela's African Nationalist Congress and Robert Sobukwe's Pan-Africanist Congress, then imprisoned the two leaders and their chief lieutenants on Robben Island in Table Bay. After a period of some uncertainty, a young Bantu, Stephen Biko, emerged as a vigorous and popular leader. As the first president of the South African Students' Organization (SASO) in the 1960s, he had come to understand that "the most powerful weapon in the hands of the oppressor was the mind of the oppressed." His response to this condition was the founding of the Black Consciousness Movement, which he regarded as "the cultural and political revival of an oppressed people," with the general goal of liberating black people "first from psychological oppression by themselves through inferiority complex and secondly from the physical oppression accruing out of living in a white racist society," as a SASO resolution put it.

Born in King William's Town, South Africa, on December 18, 1946, Bantu Stephen Biko (Bee-kaw) attended primary school there and in Lovedale, a famous missionary school for blacks before a student strike led to its being closed down. After a strong academic performance at Marianhill, a Catholic high school in Natal, Biko spent the years 1966 to 1972 at the University of Natal, with plans initially to study medicine. During that period, however, politics intervened, when his contemporaries responded to the unassuming yet firm leadership that would characterize his life from that point on.

Described as "full of charm, large and easy and gentle and courteous and humorous," Biko was by all accounts a remarkable presence even as a young man, with an impressive command of language, as his speeches and court testimony suggest. "Everyone who met Steve in good will experienced a sort of magnetism," Dr. Trudi Thomas added to her earlier description. "I attribute it to his triumphant, unassailable normality, a touchstone you were welcome to share."

When officials forced him to leave the university in 1972, Biko was already the acknowledged leader of the South African Students Organization and the Black Community Programs. As a full-time organizer, he publicized the Black Consciousness movement that he had initiated. Within the year, however, he was banned from Durban, where he had been working, and returned to his hometown to work in the same program until he was placed under further restrictions in 1975. Although he traveled extensively after that, he had to do so secretly, protected by an increasing number of followers and admirers, both black militants and white supporters.

For a man who had braved so much, at such terrible risk, the end was swift and brutal. Arrested on September 6, 1977, Stephen Biko was taken by police to a building in Port Elizabeth, Cape Province, where they bound his hands and feet to a grille and interrogated him for twenty-two hours; during that period, he was beaten so fiercely about the head that he fell into a coma and died six days later.

Two weeks later, 20,000 people traveled from all over South Africa to King William's Town to attend Biko's funeral; others were arrested, tear-gassed, and beaten by police in their attempts to join the crowd of mourners. At an inquiry into the causes of his death—in spite of convincing evidence, photographs and testimony to the contrary—the magistrate at the hearing took only one minute to rule that Stephen Biko had died of injuries endured during a scuffle. In a remarkable account of this and other events in Biko's life, Donald Woods, a white journalist, provided transcripts of Biko's trials, including the inquiry after his death; smuggled out of the country, then completed after the author and his family escaped into exile, the book—and subsequent film based upon it—gave Biko's story to the world.

Prosecuted many times during his short life for minor offenses (a common fate of activists under seige by the white political police), Stephen Biko won the respect even of those who carried out the laws perpetuating apartheid in the courtrooms and jails of his country. Among many testimonies, his eloquent defense of nine young blacks prosecuted by the country's Supreme Court in 1976 is perhaps the best known. There, as on previous occasions, he turned the courtroom into a forum for black grievances against a repressive and racist government, while at the same time defending Black Consciousness as a constructive rather than a destructive philosophy.

According to many accounts, Biko consistently separated the Nationalist mentality that subjugated him from the individuals caught up in the system. Such behavior reflected the strength and subtlety of his character, evident in many settings, as well as the strong religious influences that echoed in his speeches, interviews, and occasional writings. Not surprisingly, several tributes at the time of his death emphasized his importance not only as a political theorist, but also as a lay theologian.

Although reared an Anglican and educated in church-related schools, Biko saw African Christianity as a colonial inheritance, a product of and symbol of imperial Europe; "the mainline churches were hardly influenced by the black fact," he said. For that reason, he regarded the questioning attitude of black theology in the late 1960s as its most important contribution, challenging "not Christianity itself, but its Western package, in order to discover what the Christian faith means for our continent."

Although he had resigned from the University Christian Movement (UCM) in 1968 to form the South African Student Organization, Biko's influence is apparent in UCM deliberations regarding black theology after that. For him, black consciousness and black theology were closely related, since "a large proportion of people in South Africa are Christians still swimming in a mire of confusion—the aftermath of the missionary approach," he said in an essay published in 1973.

Black theology provided an opportunity "to bring back God" to black people, to the truth and reality of their situation. Black-consciousness-theology was a means for Black Africans to reclaim what was rightfully theirs. In this way, Biko belongs to a special company of martyrs whose leadership contributed to a religious awakening accompanying other recent movements for social change around the world.

BY STEPHEN BIKO

"Steve Biko Speaks: Our Stategy for Liberation," *Christianity and Crisis*, January 16, 1978, 329-32.

The Challenge of Black Theology in South Africa. Basil Moore, ed. Atlanta: John Knox Press (1973), 1974.

ABOUT STEPHEN BIKO

American Friends Service Committee. *South Africa: Challenge and Hope.* Lyle Tatum, ed., Rev. ed. New York: Hill and Wang, 1987.

Wilmore, Gayraud S. "Steve Biko, Martyr," *Christianity and Crisis.* October 17, 1977, 239-40.

Woods, Donald. *Biko.* New York: Paddington Press, Ltd., 1978.

CHINESE STUDENTS

Being sentenced, I will speak my piece,
saying to the world, "I accuse!"
And although you trod a thousand resisters
under foot,
I shall be the one-thousand-and-first.
—Bei Dao

AVOIDING THE LINE OF MARCH SO AS NOT TO BE BRAND-
ed "a foreign instigator," I accompanied the students and faculty

each morning in late May 1989, as they left the gates of Nanjing University to walk to Gu Lou Square at the center of the city. The Bell Tower above the square where they gathered for speeches and, eventually, a fast, was immediately recognizable to anyone in China, though not as well-known to the rest of the world as Tiananmen Square, where protests against government corruption originated several weeks before.

Deeply moved by the students' protest, their discipline and intelligence in explaining the nature of their protest to workers and townspeople, I knew—as they knew—the likely consequences of their nonviolent resistance to a repressive State. Yet even party members, including university officials, joined in the protest and publicly supported the students. Days later, groups of young people left Nanjing on "the long march" to Beijing, 700 miles north, to join their contemporaries and former schoolmates. After the June 4 massacre of students in Beijing, shot down by government troops on the edge of Tiananmen Square, however, faculty members and officials in Nanjing sent buses north to pick up the students and bring them back. Shortly afterward, university officials and Jiangsu provincial officials (governing an area the size of New York State, with 60 million people) closed the universities— a wise move to discourage intervention by the army, stationed on the outskirts of the city.

In the history of nonviolent social change, the Chinese students who initiated the campaign for reform in 1989 claim a special place. Their effort, "one of the largest and best organized nonviolent political protest movements the world has ever seen," as Orville Schell said in the *New York Review of Books* that summer, will be a subject for study and reflection by anyone seriously committed to constructing peace and to rebuilding the social order. So it is appropriate that the Albert Einstein Institution at Harvard University and peace research centers are engaged in an on-going study of the movement.

Observing those young people at close range, in Shanghai, Nanjing, and Harbin—before and after the June 4 suppression—I was often reminded of similar movements against corruption and oppression throughout the world, particularly those in the Southern United States during the height of the Civil Rights movement and in New England during resistance to the wars in Southeast Asia and the Persian Gulf.

Throughout China in the spring of 1989, as in the Southern U.S. in the winter of 1960, students gave meaning to democracy each day, taking their message to the wider community through wall posters, demonstrations, and speeches. As with those involved in voter registration in Mississippi and lunch counter sit-ins in North Carolina, young people gave voice to the hopes and grievances of their elders, many of whom had suffered previously under a repressive political system.

Although Nanjing had been the site of demonstrations in April 1989, university students in that "southern capital" (200 miles west of Shanghai, on the Yangtze River) had little formal organization prior to mid-May. During the initial stages of the protests, before being joined by thousands from other universities throughout the city, students "with their knees knocking" as one observer said, gathered at the Nanjing University gate for the first march to Gu Lou Square.

By mid-May, their contemporaries and close friends in Beijing—calling for an end to nepotism, government corruption, and press censorship—had clearly struck a note that reverberated in the hearts and minds of millions. In giving encouragement and support to students throughout the country, workers and peasants, as well as intellectuals, artists, and teachers, revived a tradition associated with another historic protest seventy years before. In the May 4 Movement, 1919, a previous generation of students had called their elders to account and by their effort had furthered the birth of modern China.

By late May 1989, people in every major city had joined the struggle with demonstrations and hunger strikes. A crowd of 100,000 people poured into the streets of Nanjing, blocking the pedicab carrying my driver, luggage, and me from the train station to the university, as I arrived from Shanghai. Quotations on posters and banners from Chinese poets, ancient and modern, as well as from Lord Acton ("Absolute power corrupts absolutely") and Martin Luther King ("I have a dream...") reflected the students' impatience with the party leadership under Deng Xiaoping and Li Peng.

Like their parents and teachers, students in Nanjing knew well the effects of inflation and wide-scale government corruption that accompanied the previous decade of economic reform. Although some people had profited by a freer market and life generally had improved for many Chinese between 1979 and 1989, people on fixed incomes had to moonlight or to dip into small savings in order to pay the rapidly increasing prices for food and clothing. Public knowledge about party officials getting rich because of their control over the distribution of goods and services had made many people openly cynical about "the old men" ruling the national government.

In earlier student protests, beginning in 1986, student slogans about democratic reform had been rather vague and grandiose. Even the demonstrations in April 1989, after the death of Hu Yaobang, an official popular among university students, were festive rather than political. By May 18, the day of my arrival in Nanjing, the demonstrations focused upon particular grievances, including a party chief's editorial denunciation of the student movement. Such a change would probably go unnoticed in many countries of the world. In China, it suggested a clarification of goals and purposes among young activists and the wider community.

In over 350 cities, as in Beijing, where a young woman, Chai Ling, had assumed leadership of the movement, many journalists working for the government-controlled media supported the students by joining the demonstrations or providing extensive coverage on radio and television—a noteworthy, if short-lived contribution to the nonviolent movement. Student successes in gaining popular support grew, as the young "intellectuals," often resented by workers and townspeople, entered and leafletted factories and workplaces, explaining their campaign to everyone. As did many adults, I admired the students' resourcefulness and restraint and their patriotic spirit. The movement grew.

By late May, faculty, including members of the Communist Party, also signed wall posters and spoke at demonstrations. For a time, the government media transmitted accurate accounts of events at Tiananmen Square and elsewhere, whetting the people's appetite for accurate information and precise details regarding reform. Then, the government imposed martial law; and although wall posters and slogans became increasingly hostile toward Li Peng, the crowds in Nanjing remained purposeful and calm in their requests that the government retract its denunciation of the student movement and initiate reforms. The movement had spread through numerous other cities to Harbin, 700 miles north of Beijing, where I attended an international conference on American literature in early June.

Then, on June 6, came the crackdown, swift and brutal, in the streets of Beijing, with threats of similar reprisals against the students and workers in other major cities. And the re-writing of history to conform to the party-line began immediately, with government news agencies jumbling dates and scenes of the army's entrance into Beijing. In interviews that appeared rehearsed, "ordinary people" gave their versions of the June 4 massacre and offered flowers and food to "heroic soldiers" who had "defended the nation" against "counter-revolutionary elements," "rascals," and "hoodlums."

Following the killings in Beijing, some people cried out for vengeance against the government, smearing the Chinese character for "blood" across wall posters, drawing caricatures of government officials as Nazis wearing swastikas, particularly after the news reached Harbin that four students from the University of Science and Technology there had died in Beijing. Such responses were understandable, but in this case, as in most others involving citizens' efforts against the State, the weapons for vengeance, for blood, are all on the government's side.

Faculty everywhere wanted no students walking directly into another senseless slaughter. Then, as now, any direct confrontation with the government seemed not only unwise, but suicidal, though the struggle for freedom of the press and an end to autocratic rule and corruption in high places continued by other means.

Among the many people I spoke with in China, before and after June 4, no one—neither Chinese nor foreigner—anticipated the brutality of the government's response. Gradually, however, people began to understand the historic, then tragic events within the context of recent history. The year before the struggle, in tracing the course of economic and political reforms since Mao's death, Harry Harding had recognized, for example, that "despite the sometimes dramatic cycles in reform since 1978, the most difficult stage in the course of China's second revolution may still lie ahead."

Although even the most pessimistic observers doubt that the government will repeat the excesses of the Cultural Revolution, executions and arrests indicate that hard-liners within the party are against supporting basic human rights for their own people. Even in the face of a widely-supported reform movement, the party was willing to openly betray its disorganization and viciousness.

Following the repression, many people outside China wondered how best to support those who had already taken such risks for political reform out of loyalty to their country and concern for its welfare. Since returning from China later that fateful summer, I often remember a Nanjing friend's response when I asked him what a foreigner might do to keep alive the memory of the students in Tiananmen Square and elsewhere. In a late-night conversation, and again before I left for Shanghai and the long flight home, he focused upon this issue: some means of transmitting information by television to the people of China, some means of reaching the millions who rely for news only on official channels with their lies and propaganda.

During the student demonstrations, rumor had it that some soldiers in Beijing with access to international news decided not to fire on their countrymen and women. According to my Chinese friend, similar incidents in India, where people tapped into Western news sources, had strengthened the public to resist oppression there. In China, anyone listening to foreign broadcasts may retain some perspective on events, in the face of the government's re-writing of history; but the return of Hong Kong to Chinese rule will further reduce peoples' access to these alternate sources of information.

"One of the worst aspects of living in brisk, dictatorial China," as Paul Theroux has said, "is that you seldom have an accurate idea of what is really going on." Where 70 percent live on the land, sources of reliable information are severely restricted. Even though students returning from the universities took word of the pro-democracy movement to their homes and communities, for example, they represent a small fraction of the population. And the nonviolent movement, particularly, depends upon broad dissemination of accurate information about issues and events. Because of its manipulation of the news, the government won a propaganda war and convinced many people that in Beijing the casualties were few. It even succeeded temporarily in re-writing the history of the movement. But too many people tasted the flavor of free speech to forget their appetite for a more open society. Or so it seems to anyone attentive to the costly victories of the students' movement in speaking truth to power.

Since 1989, the Chinese have had, once again, to face hard choices and personal sacrifices in order to keep alive the spirit of the movement. But the courage and resourcefulness essential to nonviolent social change are evident in the daily struggle of intellectuals and workers, particularly, who supported the movement. And detailed accounts of strategies employed in confrontations with the government, including the army, have already contributed to our knowledge and understanding of nonviolence in that culture. As with Martin Luther King and his associates in the civil rights movement, Chinese students learned quickly as they went along, improvising and keeping alert in the face of overwhelming odds. Finally, in desperation and cynicism, people in power resorted to murder, as they have previously in China and elsewhere.

Someday, nonetheless, a space near Tiananmen Square will undoubtedly be set apart as a memorial to these young men and women—a reminder of their gifts to the people of China and, by extension, to citizens everywhere. "The sacrifice of the students at Tiananmen Square, in all its dignity and power," Christopher Kruegler wrote in the *New York Times*, is rightly compared to that of the people who died at Amritsar in India or in Mississippi and other movements for social justice. In our hearts and memories, those young people deserve a very special place, particularly for anyone committed to the welfare of others and to nonviolent social change.

BY CHINESE STUDENTS
Li Lu. *Moving the Mountain: My Life in China.* New York: Putnam, 1990.

ABOUT CHINESE STUDENTS
Butterfield, Fox. *China: Alive in the Bitter Sea.* Rev. ed. New York: Random House, 1990.

Harding, Harry. *China's Second Revolution: Reform After Mao.* Washington, D.C.: Brookings Institute, 1987.

June Four: A Chronicle of the Chinese Democratic Uprising. Jin Jiang and Qin Zhou, transl. Fayetteville: University of Arkansas Press, 1991.

Rosemont, Jr., Henry. "China: The Mourning After," *Z Magazine.* March 1990, 85-96.

Schell, Orville. "China's Spring," *New York Review of Books.* June 29, 1989, 3-4, 6-8.

Sharp, Gene, and Bruce Jenkins. "Nonviolent Struggle in China: An Eyewitness Account," *Nonviolent Sanctions: News from the Albert Einstein Institution.* I, No. 2 (Fall 1989), 1, 3-7.

JOAN BAEZ
1941-

THE DIALOGUE BEGINS WHEN A SKEPTIC ASKS, PREDICTA-bly, "Okay, you're a pacifist. What would you do if someone were, say, attacking your grandmother?"

The respondent replies with another question: "Attacking my poor old grandmother?...I'd yell, 'Three cheers for Grandma!' and leave the room."

"No, seriously," the questioner says: "Say he had a gun, and he was about to shoot her. Would you shoot him first?"

"Do I have a gun?"

"Yes."

"No, I'm a pacifist, I don't have a gun."

The verbal ping-pong continues, until the experienced, exasperated respondent asks, "Why are you so anxious to kill off all the pacifists?"

Insisting that he doesn't want to kill off all pacifists, the questioner says he just wants to know what a pacifist would do if he or she "were with a friend driving very fast on a one-lane road approaching a dangerous impasse where a ten-month-old girl is sitting in the middle of the road with a landslide on one side of her and a sheer drop-off on the other."

Taking a deep breath, the pacifist answers satirically: "I would probably slam on the brakes, thus sending my friend through the front windshield, skid into the landslide, run over the little girl, sail off the cliff, and plunge to my own death. No doubt Grandma's house would be at the bottom of the ravine, and the truck would crash through her roof and blow up in her living room, where she was finally being attacked for the first, and last, time."

The respondent in this dialogue/essay ("Three Cheers for Grandma!") is Joan Baez, an experienced nonviolent activist with a stand-up comic's timing and wry humor. In it, she succeeds in both answering and poking fun at a question that every peacemaker faces in trivial or serious challenges to a pacifist's value system. Remembering Baez, most pacifists probably never hear the question, "What would you do if?" with the usual impatience or exasperation.

The autobiographical *Daybreak* (1968) in which Baez's essay first appeared seems surprisingly mature for someone then in her mid-twenties. Uneven as a book, nonetheless it contains some remarkable insights into the historical period and cultural forces that contributed to her early fame.

Singer, writer, peace activist, and founder of human rights organizations, Joan Baez performed in concerts for the Civil Rights movement while she was still a teenager. During that time, she was frequently pictured with Martin Luther King and others at demonstrations and benefits for justice and peace organizations around the country, when schools in the south were being integrated for the first time.

Born on Staten Island, New York, on January 9, 1941, Joan Baez is the daughter of Joan Chandos Bridge and Albert V. Baez, of English, Scottish, Irish, and Mexican descent and the Quaker persuasion. Her father, a physicist, taught at Stanford, Harvard, and M.I.T., and it was in the Boston area that Joan Baez began singing in coffee houses in the late 1950s. For awhile, she studied music at Boston University, where she took a particular interest in Anglo-American ballads and spirituals, and after regular local appearances came to the attention of folk artists Theodore Bikel and Harry Belafonte. At 18, Baez was invited to perform at the Newport Folk Festival; the enthusiastic response of the audience in Newport, Rhode Island, and subsequent performances led eventually to friendships with other well-known folk singers— Odetta, the Weavers, and Pete Seeger—all of whom were associated with movements for social change before Baez was born.

An early (1960) Baez recording has been called "the highest selling individual female folk album in the history of long-playing records"; and numerous albums, including one with Bob Dylan, followed. In 1968, Baez married David Victor Harris, a draft resister who went to federal prison for three years soon after their marriage; the parents of a daughter, they were divorced in 1973, after co-authoring a book and making a documentary film, *Carry It On*, and several other joint efforts in working to end the war in Vietnam and U.S. intervention throughout Southeast Asia.

Baez spent two brief periods in jail as a result of participation in demonstrations against the war, and endured the ferocious Christmas, 1972, bombing of Hanoi—ordered by Richard Nixon and Henry Kissinger—during her visit to North Vietnam. Although her activities, including war tax resistance and efforts on behalf of political prisoners, were less well-publicized—or less "popular"—during the late 1970s and 1980s, Baez remained faithful to values associated with nonviolent social change. As a singer, she continued to record and to conduct international tours and benefit concerts for groups committed to nuclear disarmament. In 1976, she founded the Resource Center for Non-Violence, in Santa Cruz, California, which provides public education programs on the "history, theory, methodology and current practice of non-violence as a force for personal and social change." The Center arranges visits between citizens of the U.S. and Latin American countries and counseling for conscientious objection. Later, Baez initiated Humanitas International, which focuses on human rights in Central America and supports nonviolent reforms in those countries.

Baez's popular records, books, concerts, and documentary films have brought her work to the attention of audiences throughout the world. That public attention has also complicated her life; both conservatives and liberals have attacked her in a complex and difficult period since the end of the Vietnam war. A critic of American foreign policy, she is nonetheless critical of injustices associated with foreign governments as well, and has consistently taken the side of victims under repressive regimes. During "the long sleep" of the Reagan/Bush administrations, she challenged their policies and worked for positive alternatives as a board member of Amnesty International and through the two organizations she founded.

In conducting her education in public and dealing with public criticism of her "radical" politics, while following her vocation as an artist, Baez has been remarkably frank and persistent in a dark time. She has faced some of the same conflicts and uncertainties that marked the lives of other singers in the tradition of resistance; she has clearly benefited from their contributions and the example of their lives as well.

Since at least the early 20th century, the "folk" tradition has thrived in the lives and writings of several remarkable artists, beginning with Joe Hill, an organizer for the Industrial Workers of the World (I.W.W. or "Wobblies"). A Swedish immigrant, friend of Elizabeth Gurley Flynn, "The Rebel Girl," and an activist among miners in the Rockie Mountains, Hill was killed by the State of Utah in 1915. His last words were, "Don't mourn, Organize!" He also asked his friends to cremate his body and send the ashes to workers around the world "because I don't want to be caught dead in Utah." Through her effective rendering of a song about his influence on workers and organizers, Baez is associated with the Wobblie balladeer's memory:

I dreamed I saw Joe Hill last night
Alive as you and me.
"Takes more than guns to kill a man,"
Says Joe, "I didn't die."...

"Joe Hill ain't dead," he says to me.
"Joe Hill ain't never died.
Where workingmen are out on strike,
Joe Hill is at their side."

Another major figure back of Baez is, of course, Woody Guthrie, author of thousands of songs, including "This Land Is Your Land"—which many Americans regard as our national anthem—and father of Arlo Guthrie. In *Bound for Glory* (1943), his autobiography, "Okie minstrel" Guthrie tells about the consequences of his commitment to social reform in the 1930s; and Baez's autobiographical writings bear a certain resemblance to his. Guthrie's songs have been kept alive and augmented by Pete Seeger and several of Baez's contemporaries—Phil Ochs, Utah Phillips, Charlie King.

Although not always optimistic about the consequences of her own or other people's commitment to halt the making of deadly weapons, Baez remains, as she wrote in 1986, "resilient, hopeful, determined, active, and ready to take risks." In her commitment to nonviolent social change, she combines a deeply spiritual, religious base with a direct and practical approach. In answering a traditional challenge posed by 19th century Russian radicals, including Tolstoi and Kropotkin, "What is to be done?" Baez recommends beginning modestly: (1) see Richard Attenborough's film *Gandhi* and read Martin Luther King's speeches for inspiration; (2) call a local peace organization and get involved. From there, the path that each person takes to "the peaceable kingdom" is probably unique, as hers has been.

BY JOAN BAEZ
And a Voice to Sing With. New York: Summit Books, 1987.

Daybreak. New York: Dial Press, 1968.

The Joan Baez Songbook. New York: Ryerson Music Publishers, Inc., 1964.

Voices of Survival in the Nuclear Age. Dennis Paulson, ed. Santa Barbara, Cal.: Capra Press, 1986.

What Would You Do? A Serious Answer to a Standard Question. John H. Yoder, ed. Scottdale, Penn.: Herald Press, 1983.

ABOUT JOAN BAEZ
Harris, David. *Goliath.* New York: Avon Books, 1970.

Songs of Peace, Freedom & Protest. Tom Glazer, ed. Greenwich, Conn.: Fawcett Publications, Inc., 1970.

Hard Hitting Songs for Hard-Hit People. Alan Lomax, ed. Oak, 1967.

THE SANCTUARY MOVEMENT

ACROSS THE DESERT OF SOUTHWESTERN ARIZONA SEVER-
al people walk, having left a Guatemalan or Salvadoran village
several days before. It is 1981. Earlier, they traveled by crowded
bus or car north into Mexico, then—with the help of guides
(called coyotes)—headed toward the United States. Their families
and neighbors encouraged them to leave their homeland, after
friends and associates were tortured and murdered by uniformed

death squads, after young sons from their area had been carried away as conscripts for the military. Those killed had done nothing more than read the Bible or teach catechism, with a nun and priest who had helped them form a cooperative and build a well and community shelter.

Having followed guides through a barbed-wire fence on the American border, then over a mountain range, they are now on their own, with little idea of their exact location. And they wonder, will anyone help once they reach their destination? The coyotes probably abandoned the group for several reasons. They may have thought, first of all, that this mission is doomed; and they want to avoid discovery, fearing they might lose the opportunity of offering their illicit, expensive "services" to other refugees.

Both adults and children in the group must make their way quickly, secretly. Their water supply may not hold out. What they fear most is being arrested as illegal aliens and returned to their country, since returnees are seldom heard of again. (Many are also arrested in Mexico or in the U.S. and held in prison, knowing nothing of their rights.) One thing for sure, they will never sign a form enabling U.S. Immigration and Naturalization Service authorities to send them back home....

Some variation of this story unfolded many times during the early 1980s, along the Mexican-American border from the Rio Grande Valley in Texas, across to Lower California and the Pacific Ocean. Such stories, almost a literary genre, resemble earlier ones involving black families leaving the South prior to the Civil War; Jews escaping Germany and elsewhere in Europe during the 1930s; Tibetans abandoning their homeland after the Chinese invasion and seeking refuge in India during the 1960s; and others escaping repression in this cruel century.

In a special irony, these Central American refugees fled governments that have enjoyed extensive military and economic aid from the United States; and the death squads who killed their families and neighbors are armed with weapons from, and trained by, experts at military posts in "the land of the free." Although the suffering endured by Central Americans resembles that of the world's refugees, the circumstances that provoked their suffering are peculiar. So are the events that led to the harassment endured by U.S. citizens trying to stop it.

The story of the sanctuary movement, in other words, is twofold, involving (1) landless peasants and some city dwellers facing death in Central America; and (2) "ordinary" middle-class citizens of the U.S. risking jail in order to protect them. The first part of the story, recounted above, has its origins in the structural violence of a system that keeps people illiterate and landless. The second part, discussed below, has its origins in the structural violence of a system in the U.S. that fosters ignorance and irresponsibility.

As their only hope of survival, the refugees escaped the conditions of one system by leaving their native countries. The second group, U.S. citizens of the sanctuary movement, challenged and altered slightly the conditions of the other system, as previous citizens of this country have done, by acts of courage. They resisted unjust laws and risked civil disobedience; more importantly, they built a community of support in order to correct the injustices which they had previously tolerated.

Although the American side of the story began in the Southwest, it gradually involved many areas of the U.S., as people's awareness of the conditions among refugees became known and churches, religious congregations, and households opened their doors, in states as far apart as Minnesota and Maine. As their education—a kind of radicalization—progressed, citizens of the U.S. began to make connections between themselves and their neighbors and the relationship between U.S. foreign policy and the border scene described above. As a result, they reclaimed "a preferential option for the poor," the same one to which the Latin American church had committed itself at Medellin in 1968 after the Second Vatican Council. In a more secular, political manner, U. S. citizens also reminded themselves (and others) of Thomas Jefferson's dictum that "government is for the living."

The initial response in the early 1980s to the Central Americans who showed up along the Southern Arizona border could hardly have been more modest. Local residents, even those who knew something about conditions in Central America, thought these Spanish-speaking refugees were simply Mexicans coming into the state to work. Gradually, a Quaker rancher, Jim Corbett, and clergy who had spoken with Salvadorans in prison learned why so many refugees took dangerous risks to escape their governments. By 1981, an estimated eighty Salvadorans a week, on their way to the U.S., were deported by the Mexican government. This happened as a result of a "neighborly" agreement with the U.S. government. By June of that year, Jim Corbett had talked with enough refugees to realize that rather than being illegal aliens, they were actually "political refugees, deserving political asylum in the United States," as Miriam Davidson writes in her powerful narrative about Corbett and the sanctuary movement.

Since 1981 and particularly in 1984, the year the government indicted eleven sanctuary workers for housing the refugees, the story resembles those of other ordinary Americans responding to injustice. Although the details and events reflect the peculiarities of the Reagan/Bush administration and its "war against the poor" in the U.S. and its war against "the threat" of liberation theology, sanctuary members behaved rather as residents of New England once did when they refused to obey the Fugitive Slave Law of 1850 requiring them to return slaves to their slavemasters. By yet another underground railway during the Vietnam war, ministers and teachers helped draft resisters or soldiers who were denied conscientious objector status to escape to Canada.

By its Central American policy under Reagan, the United States supported increased repression in Guatemala and El Salvador. Meanwhile, along its Southwestern border, Americans accepted the immigration office's description of the refugees as "just some more Mexican aliens" coming over the border to make money; in reality, they were political refugees with a legitimate claim—according to a United Nations ruling—to political asylum. Fortunately, some "helpers" came to the rescue of the refugees, providing sanctuary in Arizona and beyond. In doing so, they found themselves in conflict with neighbors and parishioners and formed communities of support to protect political refugees not only from some foreign despots, but from representatives of the U.S. government, particularly the Office of Immigration and Naturalization. In 1984, a judge in the Tucson Sanctuary Trial found eleven people guilty of breaking the law; in part because of the trial's visibility and public support for what the defendants had done, they were given suspended sentences. The sanctuary movement grew, and continues in the 1990s.

In resisting their government and in their arguments before the court in the 1984 trial, members said they acted within a tradition as old as the U.S. itself. As Jim Corbett argued, "From the Declaration of Independence to the trials at Nuremberg, our country has recognized that good citizenship requires that we disobey laws or officials whenever they mandate the violation of human rights. A government that commits crimes against humanity forfeits its claim to legitimacy."

In building a community of support for the refugees and in reawakening their churches, the movement has helped to bring a version of the Latin American base communities to the U.S. and to give it indigenous roots. Vicki Kemper, commenting on the 1984 trial, suggested how this community building is accomplished, often by church workers who don't necessarily know one another. The diverse group in Tucson, "with different theologies, ministries, and politics," came together and stayed together "because of their common commitment to Central American refugees, a commitment so strong that it overshadowed all their differences."

The sanctuary movement has helped those involved, as it did Jim Corbett, to discover "the church in its broadest sense" as a community "ready to respond to violations of human rights." By embodying what he calls "faith as trust" rather than "faith as belief," the movement continues to act for the good of others in its two-fold effort of resisting and rebuilding. At the same time, it has created a new model for later use, reflecting—Corbett adds— the "unique liberating power with which every person and every community is endowed."

BY THE SANCTUARY MOVEMENT
Corbett, Jim. *The Sanctuary Church*. Philadelphia: Pendle Hill, 1986.

Interviews: John Fife, Peggy Hutchison, Philip Willis Conger, Darlene Nicgorski, Jim Corbett, *Sojourners*. XV, 7 (July 1986), 20-30.

ABOUT THE SANCTUARY MOVEMENT
Davidson, Miriam. *Convictions of the Heart: Jim Corbett and the Sanctuary Movement*. Tucson: University of Arizona Press, 1988.

Golden, Renny, and Michael McConnell. *Sanctuary: The New Underground Railroad*. Maryknoll, N.Y.: Orbis Books, 1986.

Kemper, Vicki. "Convicted of the Gospel: Inside the Tucson Sanctuary Trial." *Sojourners*. XV, 7 (July 1986), 14-19.

Sanctuary: A Resource Guide for Understanding and Participating in the Central American Rufugees' Struggle. Gary MacEoin, ed. San Francisco: Harper & Row, 1985.

PENNY LERNOUX
1940-1989

AS AN INVESTIGATIVE REPORTER, SHE SOMETIMES HAD TO
wear disguises when covering stories. In order to protect her
sources from police informers, she found it necessary to meet Latin Americans in the forest or on trains or buses moving from
place to place. In Nicaragua, she dressed as a nun while docu-
menting reports of massacres by the Somoza regime. In Bolivia,
when she reported on working conditions, miners threw dyna-
mite at her, thinking women brought bad luck. In Columbia, her

life was threatened when she identified officials complicit in the drug cartel.

For over twenty years, she covered coups and revolutions, and interviewed presidents, generals, bankers, labor leaders, bishops and cardinals of the church throughout Central and South America.

In the midst of such high drama and eventual praise from her peers, Penny Lernoux remained modest, unassuming, dedicated to her profession and to the victims whose lives she documented in her reporting. In the introduction to *People of God*, she spoke movingly about what she regarded as "the most significant political development" in Latin America in recent years: "a new church of the poor" that gave hope to the impoverished masses, as it did to her as well.

Born in Los Angeles, Penny Lernoux began her career as a journalist on the *Daily Trojan* while still an undergraduate at the University of Southern California. After working for the United States Information Agency in Columbia and Brazil, she joined a California-based news service in 1964 and reported from Caracas, Buenos Aires, and—for fifteen years—Bogota, where she lived with her husband, Denis Nahum, and their daughter, Angela. As a freelance writer for major journals of opinion and author of three important books, she received numerous awards for her investigative reporting on Latin America. At the time of her death from cancer, in 1989, she was completing a book on the Maryknoll nuns and had made plans to return to live in the United States as a university teacher.

Lernoux's peers admired her authoritative reporting and "the awakening she had stirred," as Tom Fox, editor of the *National Catholic Reporter*, put it. "And she took sides—with the poor," he said. "Always factual, always thorough, she did not apologize for her partiality. And she was good at what she did. The best." The title of a cover story in *Sojourners*, in memoriam, suggests her distinctive contribution to American journalism: "Faithful to the Truth: A Journalist of Courage and Integrity."

Lernoux's work as a journalist reflected—perhaps even accounted for—a profound religious struggle within her own sensibility "in search of a different, more mature faith." Reared a Catholic, she had gone through a period of disillusionment, then reconciliation with the church, as she traced the contradictory influences of the Vatican in her region of the world from the time of the Second Vatican Council through the reign of John Paul II.

Going to Latin America in the early 1960s, she found the church allied with rich land owners and industrialists and the military. In part because of her association with Maryknoll sisters in Chile, she "became aware of and entered into another world—not that of the U.S. embassy or the upper classes, which comprise the confines of most American journalists, but the suffering and hopeful world of the slums and peasant villages." That experience changed her life and led to her commitment "to tell the truth of the poor" as best she could. And it is clear from her singular insights about the contradictory politics of the church in Latin America that she shared "the pain inflicted on the church of the poor by a Eurocentric Vatican unable to perceive the needs and gifts of other cultures." Faithfully, over two decades, she catalogued and documented the suffering resulting from those contradictions among clergy and laity in Central and South America.

Lernoux's writings reflect, also, her deepening knowledge of the continent and her growing sensitivity to the strengths and courage of the poor. Little by little, she recognized the full implications of harsh conditions sanctioned by the rich, by the church—under Vatican dicta that had "little or nothing to do with spirituality," and much to do "with a worldly desire to retain power"—and by U.S. policies toward Latin America.

Cry of the People, her first book, contains vivid, first-hand accounts of the political and religious transformation of Central and South America between the mid-1960s and the late 1970s. (A preface to the 1982 Penguin edition describes later U.S. involvement after "Reagan's disavowal of Carter's human rights policy" gave militarists "a hunting license"' to crush dissent in the region.) The book's narrative, in three parts—"Return to the Catacombs," "U.S. Intervention," and "The Awakening"—relies on stories of ordinary people who suffered and died merely because they supported the farmers' cooperatives or new sewer systems in the slums or because they reminded local militia of the commandment, "Thou shall not kill."

A representative story involved an Irish priest, Patrick Rice, who was exiled following arbitrary arrest and imprisonment in Argentina in 1976. Men in civilian clothes seized him and a parishioner as they left his shantytown chapel and took them, at gun point, to a police station. There, the men pulled the priest's shirt over his head, asked him to recite the Our Father in Latin, then beat him. "Now you'll find out that the Romans were very civilized toward the early Christians compared with what's going to happen to you," they said. Afterward they tortured him, his companion, and seven other prisoners by pouring water down their throats and applying electric shocks to various parts of their bodies. What happened to Father Rice and the others has happened to tens of thousands of people under similar governments since then.

For decades, such tactics had been used against opposition political parties and labor unions by repressive governments in Brazil, Chile, Bolivia, often by police trained in the U.S. or by military personnel armed with American weapons. After 1965, governments began employing similar tactics against the church, as the price of its commitment to the poor, in a wave of persecution of Catholics and Protestants "unparalleled in modern history, even in Hitler's Germany and Stalin's Soviet Union." By 1979, an estimated 850 priests, nuns, and bishops had been arrested, tortured, murdered, or expelled, and thousands of laity had been jailed or killed.

Lernoux regarded these changes in domestic policy by the government and in theological perspective by the church as an historical coincidence. After the Second Vatican Council, the church in Latin America began to express its concern for poor and oppressed people in new pastoral work, just as the continent became engulfed in yet another wave of military dictatorships. Clergy formerly guarded in their criticism found themselves, because of unprecedented repression against their parishioners, in open conflict with governments. In Lernoux's words, "out of adversity was emerging a socially conscious Church."

It also became a divided church, with some clergy supporting the status quo and others struggling to understand and to offer alternatives. Whichever path they followed in this "awakening" was difficult, for the way to reform is long and treacherous. In two later books, which focus on economic and religious institutions that affect human rights, Lernoux examined the institutions preventing or undermining reform.

In Banks We Trust discusses the relationship between U.S. banking systems and Latin American countries during the 1970s lending spree and the collapse of many banks following a period of speculation. In a greedy game involving OPEC oil ministers, Latin American dictators, the C.I.A.—and complicity at the highest levels in the U.S.—managers faced few restraints. Amid frequent illegal practices by the country's most respected financial institutions and panic situations in several states, hundreds of banks collapsed every year, long before the 1991 depression. Not surprisingly, as the "money-recycling" game spun out of control, with the U.S. becoming a debtor nation for the first time since 1917, the American public, then the world, lost confidence in a once impeccable financial system. With characteristic simplicity and directness, Lernoux describes the consequences of careless or unscrupulous policies that enabled crooks to launder money, evade taxes, and gouge taxpayers.

In the same period, another influential institution faced a crisis. Among Catholics, as Lernoux described them in *People of God*, competing visions of religious faith dramatized a conflict between "the church of Caesar, powerful and rich, and the church of Christ—loving, poor, and spiritually rich." In a lengthy commentary on the Catholic church in the United States, she made telling links between the Vatican's "counter reformation" in this country (the disciplining of Archbishop Hunthausen and Rev. Charles Curran) and the suppression of liberation theology elsewhere in the world. In spite of repressive forces, including "the power plays and intrigue of Rome," however, "the people of God" will persist, Lernoux argued. "And the Third World will continue to beckon to the First, reminding it of the Galilean vision of Christian solidarity."

That statement, at the end of *People of God*, published shortly before Penny Lernoux's death, returned to a theme in her first book, *Cry of the People*, which ended with these lines from W. H. Auden:

To choose what is difficult
all one's days
as if it were easy,
that is faith.

BY PENNY LERNOUX
Cry of the People: United States Involvement in the Rise of Fascism, Torture, and Murder and the Persecution of the Catholic Church in Latin America. New York: Doubleday, 1980.

Fear and Hope: Toward Political Democracy in Central America. New York: The Field Foundation, 1984.

In Banks We Trust. New York: Doubleday, 1984.

The People of God: The Struggle for World Catholicism. New York: Viking, 1989.

ABOUT PENNY LERNOUX
Wallis, Jim. "Faithful to the Truth," and Tom Fox, "A Public Journey of Faith: The Gift of Penny Lernoux," *Sojourners*, December 1989, 4-5 and 14-17.

GREENHAM COMMON WOMEN

As a woman, I have no country....As a woman, my country is the whole world.   —Virginia Woolf

THE INITIAL MEDIA RESPONSE TO THE GREENHAM COMmon Women—"the harridans of Greenham Common"—was predictable. Others expressed their hatred of women activists in similar cliches hurled at 19th century abolitionists and early feminists generally.

Remembering these and similar reports from the 1980s makes one wonder if historians may eventually regard the decade as the worst, politically, in our time. Was there ever a succession of presidential administrations in the U.S., for example, when mean-spiritedness, deception, and greed were so blatant? Has public opinion ever shown such contempt for the poor, the down-and-out, the vulnerable? Were the rich and powerful ever so crass, so unfeeling?

As billions of dollars were appropriated and spent on weapons of war—in direct proportion to the increase in homeless, hungry people—policies leading to these conditions went practically unchallenged by otherwise decent citizens. Even powerful congressional leaders regarded opposing the Reagan administration as political suicide, when the global consequences of its policies were overt and covert wars in the Middle East, Latin America, Southeast Asia, the Caribbean.

At the same time, a small band of resisters advocated alternative policies and initiated programs of public moral education. In the U.S., it included the Clamshell Alliance, the Atlantic and Pacific Life Communities. Among these and similar faithful witnesses, no one was more persistent, faithful, and imaginative than the Greenham Common Women in England. In defying the deadly duo, Reagan/Thatcher, these women initiated and maintained a decade-long campaign to halt the proliferation of nuclear missiles at an American base, "USAF Greenham Common," just south of London.

"We are not on trial. You are," Katrina Howse told the court on November 17, 1982, in Newbury, Berkshire. The power the court uses to support nuclear weapons, she continued "supports binding women's voices, binding our minds and bodies in prison so our voices cannot be heard....But we cannot be silenced. And I cannot be bound over." In addressing the magistrates, Katrina Howse joined thousands of women who had been camping on Greenham Common for over a year, protesting the largest cache of nuclear missiles in Europe.

A December 1979 decision by the North Atlantic Treaty Organization (NATO) to station 464 land-based U.S. cruise and Pershing II missiles in Europe had prompted the women's persistent daily resistance to nuclear arms on English soil. The decision to put a fourth of the weapons at Greenham Common, the women said, had been taken "over our heads and without our knowledge" and over the heads of most elected Members of Parliament. In an initial action, August 27, 1981, women, children, and men marched from Cardiff, Wales, 125 miles to the "USAF/RAF Greenham Common," near Newbury, southwest of London, to protest that decision. Arriving there, and after being denied a national debate on the issues, they set up a peace camp which eventually inspired similar projects against nuclear missiles throughout Europe.

In December 1982, a month after Katrina Howse's court appearance, 30,000 women circled the nine-mile perimeter fence and sealed off the air base. Like many other women before and since, they endured fines and jail sentences for civil disobedience after repeated attempts by local authorities to evict them by harassment and intimidation. Having previously ignored Greenham Common Women and the dangers and issues surrounding the presence of deadly weapons in their midst, the whole country took notice in 1982, and a national debate ensued. Directly and indirectly, that led to later protests against the nuclear missiles involving hundreds of thousands of people in major cities throughout Europe and over a million people in New York City and, subsequently, to East/West negotiations.

At Greenham Common, as in previous episodes in the history of nonviolence, individual women reclaimed a pacifist tradition initiated by earlier feminists and brought to life values implicit in women's resistance to war from the 18th century to the present. That tradition had its origins in the Female Auxiliary Peace Societies of the 1820s; Emily Hobhouse and her efforts to draw attention to the suffering of women and children in the Boer War; activists and writers contributing to it included the Austrian Nobel Peace Laureate Bertha von Suttner and the American essayist Charlotte Perkins Gilman.

The connections that Greenham Common Women made—in building "a movement of their own"—between feminism and pacifism, gender and war were ones that Virginia Woolf also had made in *Three Guineas* (1936). Responding to several men who had asked women about how to prevent war, "with the sound of the guns in our ears," Woolf answered:

We can best help to prevent war not by repeating your words and following your methods but by finding new words and creating new methods. We can best help you to prevent war not by joining your society but by remaining outside your society but in co-operation with its aim. That aim is the same for us both. It is to assert "the rights of all—all men and women—to respect in their persons the great principles of Justice and Equality and Liberty.

Greenham Common Women lived out these ideals in keeping a round-the-clock protest which included cultural events, meetings, and discussions at the site and a wider network of individuals and groups who supported them: the Campaign for Nuclear Disarmament, initiated by Bertrand Russell and chaired at that time by E. P. Thompson; church and union associations, which provided donations supporting the movement; and others who wrote and brought encouragement from countries around the world.

Over the decade, those who carried out this remarkable witness took the values associated with their lives and concerns as "ordinary" women and applied them to the public issues that had been taken out of their hands. In meetings and organizing manuals, which quote from their journals, they brought new insights to essential questions about their own and the world's fate. Among the records of their deliberations and reflections, two having to do with the implications of their own dreams and their experience with the press are particularly interesting.

Generalizing about what women at the camp learned about themselves and nuclear war, participants concluded that the most disturbing aspect is the way dreams "related to the very threat of destruction" that hung over their lives and the future.

The effects of nuclear weapons lie in our heads, as well as in radioactive fallout. The damage that is being done *now* to people's vision of the future and their faith in future generations is incalculable.

Elsewhere, in commenting on "the highly selective filter of information" through which journalists and editors present issues, they describe conditions that keep the general public ignorant on major political issues:

> As outside observers [reporters], usually have little information or understanding about how an action is organized or what those involved feel about it. They never admit this limitation even if they are aware of it.

In speaking to the media, women who took risks to get essential information across seldom speak "directly to the audience but through screens, which vary somewhat from editor to editor. Something of what is said gets through—more or less coherently," but it is muddled up or mixed with other, often "louder" voices: press releases from offices of the prime minister or president or others with a stake in the political status quo.

These and similar insights accompanied the women's sustained effort "to construct peace" at Greenham Common, and their history is a useful model "About Political Action in Which Each Individual Acts from the Heart," as the title of a Denise Levertov poem (quoted in Chapter 13) puts it. When people act in this manner, as these women's actions dramatized, "great energy flows from solitude,/and great power from communion."

BY GREENHAM COMMON WOMEN
Cook, Alice, and Gwyn Kirk. *Greenham Women Everywhere: Dreams, Ideals and Actions from the Women's Peace Movement.* Boston: South End Press, 1983.

ABOUT GREENHAM COMMON WOMEN
Fairbairns, Zoe, and James Cameron. *Peace Moves: Nuclear Protest in the 1980s.* London: Chatto and Windus, 1984.

Liddington, Jill. *The Road to Greenham Common: Feminism and Anti-Militarism in Britain Since 1820*. Syracuse: Syracuse University Press, 1992.

Reweaving the Web of Life: Feminism and Nonviolence. Pam McAllister, ed. Philadelphia: New Society Publishers, 1982.

Virginia Woolf and War: Fiction, Reality, and Myth. Mark Hussey, ed. Syracuse: Syracuse University Press, 1991.

MAURA CLARKE
1931-1980

ON DECEMBER 2, 1980, THE DAY THAT MAURA CLARKE, Ita Ford, and two other women would be murdered in El Salvador, a man showed one of their co-workers a death list with their names on it. "Today, this very night, we will begin," he said.

Years later, in a fitting memorial to the four women, a Long Island community in offering sanctuary to foreigners said: "As we commemorate the seventh anniversary of the deaths of the four North American women—Jean Donovan, Ita Ford, Dorothy

Kazel, and Maura Clarke, martyred in El Salvador while working for justice and peace—we publicly declare ourselves to be a community of sanctuary for refugees fleeing from Central America." In committing itself to the welfare of strangers, this community, like Maura Clarke, was responding to what its members regarded as a religious calling; and they cited a passage from the Old Testament in doing so: "If a stranger lives with you in your land, do not mistreat him/her. Count and love the person as one of your own—for you were once a stranger yourself in Egypt" (Leviticus 19:34).

By 1987, associating social justice with religious teaching had become relatively common among Catholics in the United States. Maura Clarke's religious community, on the other hand, had made that association long before. As the female "branch" of the Catholic Foreign Mission Society of America, Inc., they regarded themselves in their religious ministry more as "witnesses" than as "missionaries" in the conventional, proselytizing sense. In manner and style, the women's vocation reflects the spirit of a poem, "Pescador de Gente" ("Fisher of People") that one of them, Bernice Kita, quoted in her Guatemalan memoir:

Lord, you have looked in my eyes.
Smiling, you have spoken my name.
On the sand I have left my boat
To seek with you another sea.

You know well that I have,
In my little boat, neither gold nor sword,
But this net, and the work of my hands.

Better known as Maryknoll—the name of a hill and headquarters above the Hudson River, 40 miles north of New York City—the missionary Sisters of St. Dominic, after its founding in 1912, had sent women to China, then elsewhere in Asia, and increasingly Africa, Central and South America. It all began when several lay women volunteered to help the brothers and priests who initiated the first indigenous Catholic religious order in the United States in 1911.

By 1980, Maryknoll Sisters, numbering about 900 women, were known for their powerful though modest presence wherever their commitment to the welfare of others took them—including Chile, Guatemala, the Sudan, Mindinao, Hawaii, Appalachia, the inner-city. And because they paid attention not only to what happened among the poor, but also why it happened, they began to reflect upon and to identify the causes of people's suffering. In some instances, they addressed the injustices responsible for the causes. Not surprisingly, in countries where the military supported an elite holding 80-90 percent of their land and wealth—that is, the status quo—Maryknoll women have been among the thousands deported, imprisoned, tortured, killed.

In early December 1980, Robert E. White, U.S. ambassador to El Salvador, was told that the bodies of four U.S. women, shot in the head, had been found buried near a village in the countryside. Two of them, Dorothy Kazel, an Ursuline nun from the Cleveland area, and Jean Donovan, a lay missioner from Connecticut—who distributed food and taught catechism in a coastal village—had been at the ambassador's residence for dinner earlier in the week, before they went to pick up Maura Clarke and Ita Ford on their arrival at the airport in San Salvador. The ambassador learned later that the four women had been stopped by military personnel who raped and killed the women and threw their bodies into an unmarked grave.

Some weeks before, an army officer had threatened Clarke and Ford, who worked in a refugee camp in Chalatenango, telling them that the church was subversive because it had taken the side of the powerless. That charge was new to neither woman, for they had been working under similar circumstances in Latin America for years.

Maura Elizabeth Clarke, born in New York City in 1931—the oldest of three children of Mary and John Clarke—had been a Maryknoll sister for thirty years at the time of her death. Following high school, she had joined the religious order after a variety of other experiences: work in a department store, in summer stock, and some college study. She is remembered by her friends as "a generous, fun-loving daughter of Irish-American immigrants." Before going to El Salvador in 1979, she had served in various capacities in Nicaragua over a seventeen-year period, including as principal of a school. Her experience living in a Managua barrio, after an earthquake in the 1970s, had contributed to her defining herself increasingly as an activist rather than as a teacher.

The make-shift barrio in Managua where she lived had sprung up as a new slum; and many people with no home to return to after the earthquake simply remained there. Deciding to stay among them, Clarke and other Maryknoll sisters joined the people in marching daily to city offices in an effort to get water piped into the area. Finally, after three months, they were somewhat successful, only to face other restrictions. From that point on, Clarke decided that in addition to helping people through their suffering, she would try to address its causes as well.

In 1978-79, during an assignment with the Maryknoll World Awareness program (later Reverse Mission) in the Boston area, she discussed her change in perspective with a friend, Kathy Knight, who, visiting parishes and schools as part of the archdiocesan Peace and Justice Commission, became increasingly aware of Clarke's effectiveness as an emissary for the Nicaraguan people. "She conveyed the reality of the poor in such a loving way, the way her own heart engaged with them." Although Clarke never thought of herself as a public speaker, she gradually gained confidence and a kind of eloquence in that work, and "she counseled others by sharing her own struggles, without reservation," Knight said. The stories of the suffering in Nicaragua under the Somoza regime, however, caused Clarke great pain, particularly since her assignment in New England meant living away from them.

There, her modesty, good humor, and attentiveness to others endeared her to her co-workers and to the problem-burdened, single women she lived among in a big, old rooming house in Boston's South End. Returning to Central America in 1979, Clarke corresponded with two of the women, who received letters mailed before but delivered after her death. These and other letters, circulated at memorials, conveyed a strong sense of her character. In one of them, for example—after asking "that the peace and strength of Jesus flow with renewed torrents into your most beautiful spirit"—Clark expressed her appreciation for a friend's understanding about "the death, life experience in El Salvador." Turning to a Scripture reading for that day, she quoted from the Book of Revelation: "Sweet as honey to the mouth and bitter in the stomach." In El Salvador, she said, "the thought and desire of being one with the suffering poor is sweet, but the reality is bitter indeed." Later in the letter, in a reference to the story of Jesus walking on water, Clarke returned to her time in El Salvador: "Beginning to walk on the waves has a sense of adventure, ease, but then the thinking and darkness and grasping for Christ's hand is the reality of suffering, doubt, and struggle." But "the courage and suffering of these people never ceases to call me," she concluded.

What happened to Maura Clarke and her companions in El Salvador happened to many people in Latin America. In the midst of a powerful religious renewal, clerical and lay missioners became increasingly involved in—one might say vulnerable with—landless peasants and workers. Somewhat to their surprise at first, though with a growing realization of the consequences, missionaries from the U.S. have been victimized not only by the oligarchy's police and military forces, but by agencies of the U.S. government as well.

Jon Sobrino, a well-known liberation theologian, in a reflection written soon after their deaths, spoke about the special gift that Maura Clarke and other religious women brought to nonviolent struggle, showing "us the basis of what lives truly consecrated to God mean today. Without excessive demonstrating, without eloquent discourses," he said, they lived what they regarded as the most fundamental element of a religious vocation: service.

> In doing so, they join other women religious who have slowly gone out more and more to the most abandoned places, where others cannot or perhaps do not care to go; they have in a very real sense drawn nearer to the poor in marginated barrios, in the working people's areas and, above all, to the campesinos....[in] service of and commitment to the poor.

ABOUT MAURA CLARKE

DeMott, Stephen P. "Mission Inherited: 'Our Own Blood Spilled in El Salvador,'" *Maryknoll*. Vol. 77, No. 12 (December 1983), 36-57.

Kita, Bernice. *What Prize Awaits Us: Letters from Guatemala*. Maryknoll, N.Y.: Orbis Books, 1988.

Noone, Judith. *The Same Fate as the Poor*. Maryknoll, N.Y.: Maryknoll Sisters, 1984.

Sobrino, Jon. "The Martyrdom of Maura, Ita, Dorothy and Jean." *World Parish*, Vol. 21, Number 189 (April 1981), 1-3.

Atlantic and Pacific Life Communities and Plowshares

THEIR NEWSPAPER COMBINED THE WIT OF A COMIC STRIP and the moral clarity of Thoreau's "Civil Disobedience." Its regular feature, "Dear Gandhi: Now What?"—letters and responses in the manner of "Dear Abby"—gave members of the Ground Zero Center for Nonviolent Action, in Washington state, "a way of laughing at ourselves and our ridiculous efforts to learn simple things":

Dear Gandhi,
As a chaplain in the U.S. Navy, I would like your advice on
how to preach on Jesus' teaching, "Love your enemies," to
the crew members of a Trident submarine.

> Sincerely,
> Preacher at Sea

Dear Preacher at Sea,
Give each of them a conscientious objector discharge appli-
cation; then fill one out yourself.

> Gandhi

To a reader inquiring about his preference in a presidential
election, "Gandhi" offered this advice:

If he were to run, I would vote for Winston Churchill. Winston is remembered well by the people of your country, and
he has now given up cigars, war, and imperialism. Perhaps
you can find a candidate there who has done the same.

The Ground Zero Center began as a project of the Pacific Life
Community, "a small intentional community committed to resisting the coming of Trident [nuclear submarines] to the Pacific
Northwest." As with similar resistance groups across the country,
it originated in a simple, courageous act—in this case, Robert Al-
dridge's resignation from his job as a Lockheed missile designer
in 1975 in protest against the building of nuclear weapons systems.

Two years later Jim and Shelley Douglass, creators of "Dear
Gandhi," and seven others purchased land next to a Trident base
in Bangor, Washington, and committed themselves to a long-term
presence on navy-dominated land near Stategic Weapons Facility
Pacific (SWFPAC), a nuclear weapons storage center. Fifteen
miles across Puget Sound from Seattle, hidden from public view
in a heavily wooded area, SWFPAC was circled by high-intensity
and double security fences and "patrolled 24 hours a day by Ma-
rines armed with dumdum bullets and authorized to use 'deadly
force.'"

The Ground Zero community "wanted to experiment with Gandhi's idea that the enemy has a piece of the truth, and with the religious teaching of love for the enemy. We wanted to walk the fine line between hating the sin and loving the sinner, recognizing that we, too, were complicit in violence and thus also sinners," the Douglasses later said. Their witness led to various projects, occasionally to jail, and to other people forming networks to resist the deployment of nuclear submarines and weapons.

What began in the Seattle area extended south and east along various routes that carried deadly weapons systems to the rest of the world by land and sea. In 1982, a Peace Blockade, for example, placed forty people in fifteen small boats and two 50-foot sailboats in the path of the *USS Ohio*, the first Trident submarine, as it entered the Bangor, Washington, naval base. Shortly afterward, the Agape Community grew up along train routes carrying hundreds of warheads and missile motors from the Pantex Plant in Amarillo, Texas, north and west to Utah and Washington, to be assembled in Bangor.

Over a fifteen-year period—and at present—members of the Pacific Life Community have endured arrest and jail for their persistent effort to halt the shipment of deadly weapons. A particularly dramatic incident in its history occurred in 1987, when Brian Willson, a Vietnam veteran from up-state New York, suffered harsh consequences for "making peace." As he lay across the tracks at Concord, California, Naval Weapons Station, a 250,000 pound locomotive carrying arms going to Central America crashed into him. The naval train crew ran over him, rather than remove him from danger. Surviving and eventually walking again, with the help of new prosthetic legs, Willson wrote, ironically, that he enjoyed "more 'standing' as a peace wager" after the accident than before:

The experience of standing up to the death train and wondering what my survival means has left me with a metaphysical and spiritual consciousness beyond my capacity to put in words. I feel more liberated than ever to share the gift of life....I am more committed than ever to wage unconditional peace with the empowering force of nonviolence.

On the East Coast, during the same period, the Atlantic Life Community, a similar network of spiritually-based resistance communities, initiated nonviolent actions for disarmament at the Pentagon, the White House, and various nuclear weapons research centers. With Jonah House, Baltimore, as a focal point, the community now extends south to Florida and north to Maine, and includes artists, teachers, psychiatrists, carpenters, clergy, grandmothers, students.

In 1980, several members of the Atlantic Life Community carried out the first Plowshares action, symbolically disarming MX missiles by hammering their nose cones at the General Electric facility in King of Prussia, Pennsylvania. The subsequent trial (about which a movie with Martin Sheen was made) involved eight defendants: Philip Berrigan, Daniel Berrigan, S.J., Carl Kabat, O.M.I., John Schuchardt, Dean Hammer, Elmer Maas, Anne Montgomery, R.C.S.J., and Molly Rush. The group's name had been suggested by these lines from the Old Testament prophet, Isaiah:

> And they shall beat their swords into plowshares,
> and their spears into pruning hooks;
> nation shall not lift up sword against nation
> neither shall they learn war any more.

By 1992, forty Plowshares groups, unfurling banners on warships and pouring blood on plans for other "peacekeepers," entered various weapons facilities along the East Coast, from Maine to Florida, throughout the Midwest and Southwest, and in England, Germany, and Australia. On Easter Sunday, 1991, at 3:45 A.M., for example, the five Aegis Plowshares—Kathy Boylan, Tom Lewis, Barry Roth, Philip Berrigan, and Daniel Sicken—climbed onto the *U.S.S. Gettysburg*, harbored at Bath, Maine, hammered on missile launchers, poured blood, and unfurled banners across the gunmounts. They also posted an indictment charging President Bush and other military chiefs with violations of religious, domestic, and international law in deploying weapons of mass destruction, such as the Tomahawk missiles. Then, for an hour, the Aegis Plowshares tried to find the personnel who were supposed to guard the lethal weapons.

In exposing the dangers of possessing such weapons, accessible to anyone looking for them, the Plowshares have repeatedly pointed to a major liability of the nuclear game: our vulnerability before weapons that adventurers peddle for a fast buck, at everyone else's expense around the world.

Plowshares actions resulted, of course, in arrests and sometimes long imprisonment for those who took the risks of disarmament; they also led to extensive public education about the arms race. Periodicals such as *Year One* and *Plowshares Newsletter*, several books, and documentary films provide the background information and tell the remarkable stories of people going to prison, of courtroom victories and losses, and of a faith sustained by study, work, prayer. At their trials, scholars, clergy, and public figures such as Howard Zinn, Dr. Robert Jay Lifton, Richard Falk, and Ramsey Clark testified as expert witnesses on the American tradition of civil disobedience in the public interest, from the Boston Tea Party through the Civil Rights movement. In time, Fred A. Wilcox, an historian of the movement, wrote, "our grandchildren and great-grandchildren will study Plowshares activists as we now do Harriet Tubman, Sojourner Truth, Martin Luther King, Jr., and Mahatma Gandhi," who were also loved and hated during their lifetimes. In some cases, public support led to charges being dropped against Plowshares, as they were in Maine.

Moving testimonies by Plowshares defendants justifying their actions are a particularly impressive part of this history. The principal justification, in legal terms, emphasizes "the necessity" of the actions for the protection of future generations and the environment. Yet in acting on behalf of all of us, the Plowshares recognize, as Paul Kabat, O.M.I., a defendant in the February 1985 trial, Kansas City, Missouri, did, that their chances for "success" in stopping the arms race are slim. Responding to a frequently-asked question about the effectiveness of his actions, he said:

In spite of my fantasies I do not expect my act or my resulting years in prison to have any cosmic effect on history, just as I am aware that the quiet deaths of many children in Fourth World situations around the world do not make any real difference to us Americans or to the political and economic leaders of our nation. Millions of children phase out silently and are buried in obscurity. So also, the Silo Pruning Hooks will not be much noted as time and events go by.

One might say of Father Kabat, as of other resisters, what Garry Wills once said of the Jonah House Community: "These are people who simply will not be defeated—who see the world in the bleakest terms, yet sustain most preposterous hope." Commenting on one of its favorite sayings—"The truth will make you odd," by Flannery O'Connor, Wills added, "the truth has not made enough of us odd enough to question the terrible assumptions of our age."

The Atlantic and Pacific Life Communities and the Plowshares, by contrast, not only question "the terrible assumptions" of the war-making state; they offer radically different assumptions, new beginnings. As with earlier nonviolent movements for social change, they build simultaneously what Robert Bly called "small communities of the saved."

BY ATLANTIC AND PACIFIC LIFE COMMUNITIES AND PLOWSHARES

Berrigan, Philip, and Elizabeth McAlister. *The Time's Discipline: The Beatitudes and Nuclear Resistance.* Baltimore: Fortkamp Publishing Co., 1989.

Douglass, James. "A Nonviolent Activist," and Molly Rush, "A Grandmother and Activist," in *Peace-makers: Christian Voices from the New Abolitionist Movement.* San Francisco: Harper & Row, 1983.

Douglass, Jim and Shelley. *Dear Gandhi: Now What?: Letters from Ground Zero.* Philadelphia: New Society Publishers, 1988.

Swords Into Plowshares: Nonviolent Direct Action for Disarmament. Arthur J. Laffin and Anne Montgomery, eds. New York: Harper & Row, 1987.

Wilcox, Fred A. *Uncommon Martyrs: The Plowshares Movement and the Catholic Left.* Reading, Mass.: Allison-Wesley, 1991.

Willson, Brian. "From Brian Willson," *The Plowshares Newsletter.* Vol. 5, No. 1 (Spring 1988), 1.

ABOUT ATLANTIC AND PACIFIC LIFE COMMUNITIES AND PLOWSHARES

Wills, Garry. "Inside the Whale." New York *Times*, April 1989.

Peacework: 20 Years of Nonviolent Social Change. Pat Farren, ed. Baltimore: Fortkamp Publishing Co., 1991.

Noam Chomsky
1928-

WAS EMILY DICKINSON SPEAKING TO CRITICS OF U.S. FOR-
eign policy (during the Cold, Korean, Vietnam, and Persian Gulf
wars), when she wrote:

'Tis the Majority
In this, as All, prevail-
Assent-and you are sane-
Demur-you're straightway dangerous-
And handled with a chain-

Hearing Noam Chomsky ridiculed for criticizing C.I.A. interventions and the government's disregard for human rights at home and abroad, I was reminded of Dickinson's warning. Since 1990, however, the general public is less tolerant of government wrong-doing; and information formerly confined to Chomsky's books, columns, and speeches has appeared even in the *New York Times* and on popular news programs, such as *20/20*.

Until recently, the response to Chomsky's political writings by government "experts" and academic theorists unwilling to look beyond platitudes had been predictably fierce. And commentators in the mass media who seldom imagined or offered political choices beyond (a) and (b) have ignored Chomsky's persistent consideration of (c), (d), (e), (f), and (g). What his critics could not imagine or consider was, to them, "outrageous" (as Gore Vidal, whose insights are similarly dismissed, once put it).

Born in Philadelphia, December 7, 1928, Noam Avram Chomsky is the son of Elsie Simonofsky and William Chomsky, a Hebrew scholar and teacher who immigrated to the U.S. from Russia in 1913. Educated in private and public schools, Noam Chomsky was a junior fellow at Harvard University and, in 1955, completed a Ph.D. degree at the University of Pennsylvania. Since then, he has taught at the Massachusetts Institute of Technology, where he holds a chair in modern languages and linguistics, and for brief periods at other universities in the U.S. and abroad. Married and the father of three children, he has been honored by scholarly societies and universities in this country and abroad, and inevitably draws large crowds in speaking about the foreign policy of his own and other governments. The London *Times*, in referring to him as one of the "makers of the twentieth century," reflects the opinion of contemporary historians regarding his interests and influence.

Chomsky has said that his anarcho-socialist politics were formed by "the radical Jewish community in New York"; those political enthusiasms, in turn, led him to the study of linguistics. As a young man, he took a particular interest in Jewish culture and traditions, and considered moving to Israel. Since 1965, however, he has become one of the principal critics of the American-Israeli alliance, finding the Jewish state no more reliable than other nation-states in its handling of domestic and foreign affairs.

Although clear about options and opportunities available to us for escaping economic and political disaster, Chomsky remains pessimistic about any chance of our choosing them. "What is lacking, primarily, is imagination and will," he has said. A major task involves our confronting a political system "designed to induce passivity, to make it appear that what happens in the world is beyond our control." While hoping that we might overcome perceptions about being powerless in the face of "some current Great Satan," or other "grand and impersonal forces," he doubts that we will.

A man with a healthy anarchist skepticism toward the state and a strong stomach for bad news, Noam Chosmky has undoubtedly saved many lives by "exposing the bastards" responsible for injustice in their dirty little corners of the world, in his dogged, informative investigative research on American foreign policy. Persistent, he has taken risks in order to remain unrelentingly intellectual and rational in an age and culture that is highly anti-intellectual and irrational. When the military-industrial-university complex reigned supreme in the 1980s, he shouted "The emperor has no clothes!" until that nakedness became apparent to others who eventually joined Chomsky in a public chorus. Throughout the "long sleep" that accompanied the Cold War, he has acted, spoken, and written with what Francis Hope calls "a proud defensive independence," retaining a writer's hatred of obfuscation and resisting the platitudes of contemporary thought.

Now regarded as an important social critic, Chomsky took his place among the most influential linguists in the world with the publication of a "pale blue book" called *Syntax Structures* (1957). Using a mathematical model, he constructed a system of generative grammar, a kind of "universal" grammar of languages. Throughout, he has emphasized the difference between "surface structures," applying to sounds and words in our sentences, and "deep structures," having to do with how we derive meaning from them. His sense of a linguistic order among a multiplicity of languages is reflected in theories that have influenced not only the way languages are now taught, but also the way we define ourselves as human, as Daniel Yergan once said.

Since the early, highly technical treatises on linguistics, he has also written less technical essays exploring the implications of studying language for disciplines such as psychology and philosophy. His speculative and personal Whidden Lectures, published in *Reflections on Language* (1976), for example, talk about language as "a mirror of mind," as "a product of human intelligence created anew in each individual by operations that lie far beyond the reach of will or consciousness." In suggesting similarities between the growth of language and the development of a bodily organ, Chomsky considers new ways of thinking about thinking and of understanding interactions among language, mind, and other mental organs. In this sense, his impulse to challenge preconceptions about language, which brought him first to public attention, resembles the impulse that led him, later, to challenge preconceptions about political and international affairs in his extraordinarily ambitious, prodigiously documented critiques.

American Power and the New Mandarins (1969), his first book on that topic, introduced a theme that reappears in his later writing and speaking. In that book, he calls bureaucrats and scholars trained by and often housed by the universities "the new mandarins," that is an elite—perhaps even an aristocracy—that tolerates and defends the right of the United States to dominate the globe. Quoting Randolph Bourne, the American literary radical who excoriated American intellectuals for their uncritical endorsement of America's entering World War I, Chomsky takes contemporary intellectuals to task for similar irresponsibilities in their complicity with the State and in their refusal to "speak truth to power."

Chomsky's political journalism and social criticism since *American Power and the New Mandarins* document that charge, with further examples and extensive footnotes. Their common theme is provided by George Orwell's comment, quoted at the beginning of *The Political Economy of Human Rights:* "The nationalist not only does not disapprove of atrocities committed by his own side, but he has a remarkable capacity for not even hearing about them."

Citing facts and beliefs, statistics and examples in that two-volume study, Chomsky and Edward S. Herman describe the consequences of irresponsible and immoral behavior by leaders and their gullible, sometimes willfully ignorant followers. Discussing relations between the United States and the Third World, the authors focus on domestic institutions, including the mechanisms of propaganda, that cushion any criticism of U.S. policy. Actively supporting that policy are (1) international businesses that "stifle unions and contain reformist threats" that might interfere with their exercise of power; (2) bankers and industrialists who welcome a new fascist order that suppresses dissidents, priests, labor leaders, peasant organizers. Such people serve as functionaries "playing their assigned roles in a system that has worked according to choice and plan."

Anyone choosing Noam Chomsky's way of taking on the military/industrial/university complex has heavy work cut out for him or her. After the death of Paul Goodman, who joined him in initiating a national organization challenging illegitimate authority, RESIST, Chomsky inherited the mantle of the-critic-that-others-love-most-to-misrepresent. This happened during a "popular" war when Chomsky called U.S. intervention in the Persian Gulf a "protection racket for the rich folk" and said that the transition Saddam Hussein went through (from "friend" to "Hitler") was one that many dictators had gone through before. "They're all fine as long as they're our thugs."

In the thick of battle, on the platform or the op-ed page, Chomsky is usually remarkably restrained, even discrete—yet persistent, unrelenting. In subsequent writings, he continues to expose the deceit that enables callous or thoughtless leaders to impose their will on vulnerable people.

BY NOAM CHOMSKY
American Power and the New Mandarins. New York: Random House, 1969.

The Chomsky Reader. James Peck, ed. New York: Pantheon, 1987.

The Fateful Triangle: The U.S., Israel and the Palestinians. Boston: South End Press, 1983.

Language and Mind. New York: Harcourt, Brace, 1968, 1972.

Language and Problems of Knowledge: The Managua Lectures. Cambridge, Mass.: M.I.T Press, 1988.

Necessary Illusions: Thought Control in a Democratic Society. Boston: South End Press, 1989.

(and Edward Herman) *The Political Economy of Human Rights: The Washington Connection and Third World Fascism,* Vol. I; and *After the Cataclysm: Postward Indochina and the Construction of Imperial Ideology.* Vol. II. Boston: South End Press, 1979.

Voices of Survival in the Nuclear Age. Dennis Paulson, ed. Santa Barbara, Cal.: Capra Press, 1986.

ABOUT NOAM CHOMSKY
Leiber, Justin. *Noam Chomsky: A Philosophic Overview.* Boston: Twayne Publishers, 1975.

Lyons, John. *Noam Chomsky.* New York: Viking, 1970.

Thinkers of the Twentieth Century. Gale Publishing Co., 1983.

Dolores Huerta
1930-

and

Cesar Chavez
1927-

THE SCENE: 1000 WORKERS DEMONSTRATE LEGALLY against Vice President George Bush in front of the St. Francis Hotel, San Francisco, in August 1988. Earlier, presidential candidate Bush appeared on television with California's Republican governor eating grapes, ridiculing Cesar Chavez, farm workers, and a grape boycott. Dolores Huerta, vice-president of the United Farm

Workers (UFW), responded by saying, "Mr. Bush's statement demonstrates again that he is wealthy and comfortable and insensitive to the struggles of working people in our country. It also reveals his ignorance of the pesticide threat to our environment and our people."

Minutes after she handed out this statement, policemen wielding three-foot batons plunged into the crowd of farm workers and beat Dolores Huerta, five-feet-two-inches tall and weighing 110 pounds, and Howard Wallace, a fellow organizer, in what he later called "a harrowing, terrifying experience." Fortunately for their adversaries, all farm workers had made an absolute commitment to nonviolence years ago. "Nonviolence is a total commitment," Huerta once said. "This is where women are particularly important, because they are preservers."

Following the beating, Huerta ended up in the hospital with a ruptured spleen and fractured ribs. "No one realized how serious her injuries were at first," said Richard Chavez, husband of the middle-aged mother of eleven and grandmother of ten. Within weeks after her release from the hospital, Huerta traveled the country again, in an organizing effort to stop farm owners from using dangerous pesticides in fields worked by union members.

The sacrifice of Huerta and other farm workers—including Nan Freeman, Nagi Daifallah, and Rufino Contgreras, all of whom died in *la causa*—dramatizes the high cost of their commitment to nonviolence; it helps to explain, also, why the movement has inspired workers all over the world in their struggles for decent wages and working conditions, health care, and personal dignity.

Born in Dawson, New Mexico, in 1930, the daughter of farmworker parents, Dolores Huerta moved to California as a young woman. As with Cesar Chavez, her early years as an organizer began with the Community Service Organization, which used the methods of Saul Alinsky, a well-known community organizer in the Chicago area. Alinsky once summarized his principles in a brief manifesto: "No decisions by outside elites; no demagoguery, bombast, or empty threats; rather a long series of small meetings in private homes, gradually joining in a larger structure." (Gandhi had used similar methods when he returned to India in 1915 after the successful campaign in South Africa; so did the leaders of religious reform in Latin America as they formed base communities in the early 1960s.)

Through Fred Ross, her boss in the Community Service Organization, Huerta met Cesar Chavez. In 1962, impressed by the "quiet and unassuming" Chavez, she left C.S.O. to help build the farm worker's union, becoming its first vice-president in 1965. She has remained in that post ever since, serving as a chief negotiator, lobbyist, spokesperson, and strategist. Moving from place to place, Huerta spent less than two months in any location. Characteristic assignments included tours during national boycotts of the United Farm Workers when she traveled throughout New England and spoke as a homilist at a Mass and about nonviolence during conferences of the New England Catholic Peace Fellowship at the Mont Marie, Sisters of St. Joseph, Holyoke, Massachusetts, in 1975, and Mount Holyoke College, in 1990, respectively.

In discussing the origins of the United Farm Workers, historians point to similarities between the UFW and other important campaigns for justice in American history. Leadership of effective movements for social change "need not arise from the persons most likely to benefit from it," wrote Joan London and Henry Anderson. Primary leadership for abolishing slavery, for example, "did not and could not come from slaves"; nor did children initiate the movement to abolish child labor. There is a "fine justice," nonetheless, in the way leadership for the United Farm Workers was assumed by people who were themselves the aggrieved ones. Huerta, Cesar Chavez, and other Chicanos (Mexican-Americans) worked in the fields as they organized, lived as farm workers live, and suffered the risks of their difficult lives. Even now, after long experience and an occasional victory, the leaders all look and sound and talk, not as managers or "experts," but as farm workers do.

Cesar Estrada Chavez, like his famous co-worker, is the child of farm-worker parents. Born March 31, 1927, near Yuma, Arizona, in the North Gila Valley, he lived for several years on a farm homesteaded by his grandfather, a refugee from the Mexican revolution. Then came the Depression, "the invisible scar." After losing his farm to a local banker in 1938, Cesar's father was forced to move from place to place, while he, his wife, and children worked as itinerate farmers picking vegetables and fruits in Arizona and California.

During this period, which he described so eloquently to Studs Terkel later, Chavez endured many of the humiliations that make up the life of an intinerate worker's child. He remembered one occasion in particular when his parents drove with the six children through Indio, California, and stopped at a small, road-side restaurant, its window-sign reading "White Trade Only." Chavez's father, who read English without quite understanding the meaning, walked in with "a pot he had, to get some coffee for my mother."

He asked us not to come in, but we followed him anyway. And this young waitress said, 'We don't serve Mexicans here. Get out of here.' I was there, and I saw it and heard it. She paid no more attention. I'm sure for the rest of her life she never thought of it again. But every time we thought of it, it hurt us. So we got back in the car and we had a difficult time trying—in fact, we never got the coffee.

During those years, Chavez and his brothers attended, by their own count, thirty-seven elementary schools. "We never got a transfer. Friday, we didn't tell the teacher or anything. We'd just go home...."

I remember one teacher—I wondered why she was asking so many questions. (In those days anybody asked questions, you became suspicious. Either a cop or a social worker.) She was a young teacher, and she just wanted to know why we were behind. One day she drove into the camp. That was quite an event, because we never had a teacher come over. Never. So it was, you know, a very meaningful day for us....This I remember....This is the truth, you know. History.

During the Second World War, Chavez enlisted in the navy and spent two years on a destroyer escort in the Pacific theater. Following the war, he returned to San Jose, California, where he had worked earlier, and married Helen Favila. They settled in San

Jose "on the wrong side of the tracks" with his in-laws, and worked in the fields. "We figured later that the whole family was making twenty-three cents an hour." In the off season, he took odd jobs; in 1949 the first of their eight children was born.

In the 1950s, Cesar Chavez met a priest who taught him about the social encyclicals of the Catholic church, beginning with Leo XIII's *Rerum Novarum* (1891)—on the rights of workers. In 1962, after ten years with Fred Ross and the Community Service Organization, Chavez left San Jose for Delano, California, to organize the National Farm Workers Association (NFWA), with Dolores Huerta. Both with young—and sizable—families, they took great risks, without any financial assistance from outsiders. In 1963, for example, Chavez turned down a well-paying administrative job with the Peace Corps in South America.

In time, more people, including Catholic clergy and young professionals, came forward to help in organizing and providing services for the farm workers. Through a series of events, in what came to be called "the Delano movement," workers initiated a successful rent strike. In this and a later strike against Schenley Industries, Inc., they began to claim their right to organize, a right not extended to itinerate workers by earlier federal legislation.

Finally, by 1965, the farm workers began to get help from the larger unions, including Longshoremen and Teamsters, who had ignored or actively resisted them earlier: three years, yet still so much to do and many sacrifices to make; three years—now thirty years—and the struggle continues.

In the meantime, Huerta, Cesar Chavez, their associates, and thousands of people from every background—students, journalists, nuns, doctors, clergymen, lawyers, secretaries—keep up the struggle. Some have left the movement to take up political careers or to follow other vocations; others continue to work as full-time volunteers, receiving room, board, basic expenses, and $5 a week spending money. Others give a couple of evenings a week or a full day to organize meetings, circulate petitions, write circulars, stand in picket lines at local supermarkets, or to perform basic tasks essential to carrying on a workers' campaign.

Chavez has said that a national campaign will succeed if only ten or eleven percent of the people support it. Changing the world, in other words, requires the assistance (or resistance) not of every single person, but of a conscientious, committed minority. The United Farm Workers, as with civil rights and similar movements around the world, requires, also, a disciplined, faithful leadership. Chavez still fasts periodically, as he did for 36 days just prior to the incident involving Huerta in San Francisco. "The fast is the heartfelt prayer for purification and strengthening for all of us," Chavez said afterward, "an act of penance for those of us in moral authority." All the while, adversaries, including agribusinesses linked to national or international corporations have enormous power on their side.

For all these reasons, efforts on behalf of the workers are on-going, even as the union enjoys occasional major and minor victories along the way. Through it all, Chavez, Huerta, and their associates have reason to celebrate the United Farm Workers' success in maintaining the dignity of various minorities and assisting other workers in claiming theirs.

BY DOLORES HUERTA AND CESAR CHAVEZ
"Acceptance Speech by Cesar Chavez Upon Receipt of Gandhi Peace Award, 11 May 1989," Promoting Enduring Peace, P.O. Box 5103, Woodmont, Connecticut 06460.

Hard Times: An Oral History of the Great Depression. Studs Terkel, ed. New York: Random House, 1970, 1986.

ABOUT DOLORES HUERTA AND CESAR CHAVEZ
Hope, Marjorie, and James Young. *The Struggle for Humanity: Agents of Nonviolent Change in a Violent World.* Maryknoll, N.Y.: Orbis Books, 1977.

London, Joan, and Henry Anderson. *So Shall Ye Reap: The Story of Cesar Chavez and the Farm Workers' Movement.* New York: Thomas Y. Crowell, 1970.

Mathiessen, Peter, *Sal Si Puedes.* New York: Random House, 1970.

MICHAEL HARRINGTON
1928-1989

IN THE SUMMER OF 1989, SHORTLY BEFORE MICHAEL Harrington died of cancer, John Cort asked Harrington what he would say when he found himself face to face with God, in heaven, among his old Christian friends (Harrington, brought up Catholic, regarded himself as an atheist). "I will ask Him why He mumbled," Harrington answered. Although unbelieving, Harrington nonetheless regarded God as "one of the most important political figures in Western history" whose dying "marks the rending of the social fabric."

As with anyone familiar with the religious, political, and cultural crises of his age, Harrington might well think that God had a lot of explaining to do. As a relatively unknown writer thrust suddenly into the lime-light during John F. Kennedy's administration, Harrington had conveyed tellingly and vividly, in non-fiction prose, "what the century had written on" him. In his "social autobiography" and numerous other works, he indicated the price he paid for living in a cruel century, while commiting himself to a responsible, exemplary, even inspiring vocation, as advocate for the poor and champion of economic justice, as writer and intellectual, political activist and socialist.

Harrington had a particular talent for making visible and understandable what seemed invisible and confused to his contemporaries. He saw and described vividly "The Invisible Land," as he called it, in the first chapter of *The Other America: Poverty in America* (1962): "Tens of millions of Americans are, at this very moment, maimed in body and spirit, existing at levels beneath those necessary for human decency." Everything about the poor, he recognized, "from the condition of their teeth to the way in which they love is suffused and permeated by the fact of their poverty." How quickly Americans appear to have forgotten or buried this information, only twenty years after the appearance of Harrington's powerful tract. They have forgotten in spite of Harrington's persistent cry until his death, though within two years, in the midst of a recession, they appear to be hearing it again.

The principal direction of Michael Harrington's life is best suggested in his remarks in the prologue to *Fragments of the Century:*

> I was born on February 24, 1928, in St. Louis, Missouri, the son of a gentle lawyer who fought in France during the First World War and an idealistic mother who is a teacher and educator. My childhood was spent in a happy and secure middle-class home during the Great Depression, and though I vaguely recall breadlines and the shiny union buttons on the caps of truck drivers, it is from afar. I grew up in a pleasant Irish Catholic ghetto, which made the death of God particularly poignant for me.

Returning to St. Louis as a social worker after completing an M.A. in English in 1948, he had a kind of epiphany visiting an area inhabited by sharecroppers and migrants, walking through "a decayed, beautiful house, near the Mississippi River which stank of stopped up toilets, dead rats, and human misery." He decided to devote his life "to putting an end to that house and all that it symbolized," and shortly afterward left St. Louis and...

blundered upon the end of Bohemia in New York and Paris and other cities. In the years of Cold War repression I joined a miniscule radical movement which helped me to see working people, the poor, and blacks at a time when sensible, pragmatic thinkers treated them as if they were invisible. As a result I was an early, if quite modest, participant in the struggles led by Martin Luther King, Jr., in the formation of the New Left in the sixties, and in the campaign against the war in Vietnam.

As a conscientious objector during the Korean War and as a socialist who regarded capitalism as immoral, Harrington nonetheless maintained his distance from the Students for a Democratic Society. And in 1965, somewhat undone by his sudden fame, he suffered a nervous breakdown. This ended his speaking engagements for several years, but he continued to write on a wide range of political and cultural issues. From the early 1970s until his death he worked hard, as national chairman of the Socialist party, on the Democratic Socialist Organizing Committee, and, after 1981, as co-chair of the Democratic Socialists of America (D.S.A.), to mend the splits among socialist, leftist, and liberal groups.

During the Reagan/Bush administrations, as the rest of the country moved toward the "politics of greed," support for socialism declined; one might say of D.S.A. what Harrington had said earlier of the Young Socialists League, "We could not...overthrow the Fourteenth Street subway stop on the Seventh Avenue line."

He remained, nonetheless, a visible spokesman for libertarian causes and an articulate "opposition voice" in political forums and on public radio. "His regular commentaries on National Public Radio," Jim Wallis wrote at the time of Harrington's death, "were an oasis in the parched media desert—always crackling with energy, sanity, and compassion." "To be a radical is, in the best and only decent sense of the word, patriotic," Harrington said, and remained faithful to that calling to the end. Although he knew that much of the hard work for New Deal social reforms and programs needed redoing, his optimism remained, even during the two-year illness leading to his death.

"I *should* be dejected," Harrington said in 1974, since "my life [seems to] describe a vicious circle: from the social neglect of Dwight Eisenhower through the hopes awakened by John Kennedy and the Lyndon Johnson of 1964 and 1965, then back again to the social neglect of Richard Nixon...[and Ronald Reagan]."

> I *should* be dejected, but I am not. There is a revolution that proceeds apace at this very moment, even if the President of the United States and the disillusioned intellectual refugees from the Left do not recognize it. It is not that linear progression of confrontations and battles at the barricades dreamed by romantics in the sixties, which the newly sobered thinkers of the seventies now believe was a chimera. It is not a vogue, like long hair and rock music. It is transforming our psyches and spirits and even the way our eyes see, as well as our politics and economics.

In his later books and articles, Harrington made it clear that his efforts were on behalf not of some assured triumph, but as a wager on some "sure to be unprecedented future."

The influence of his association with the *Catholic Worker*, on Manhattan's Lower East Side, remained significant in Michael Harrington's life and thought; even after he became a "religious atheist," his writing carried the marks of his friendships during and after his two years as associate editor of the newspaper, following undergraduate and graduate study at the College of the Holy Cross, Yale Law School, and the University of Chicago. In his early and most famous book, *The Other America*, he acknowledged that influence: "It was through Dorothy Day and the Catholic Worker movement that I first came into contact with the terrible reality of involuntary poverty and the magnificent ideal of voluntary poverty."

Later, many of Harrington's radical friends, including Christian anarchists and young activists during the 1960s, disagreed with his politics—with good reason, they would say—as he came to endorse policies close to the political mainstream in the Democratic party. Yet throughout his life, he remained on friendly terms with radicals and conservatives alike, always willing to debate disagreements seriously and openly. To the very end, he retained a deep interest in and commitment to students, teaching at Queens College, City University of New York, for almost twenty years, and speaking on numerous campuses in this country and abroad.

Werner Brion, a student activist at Assumption College, for example, told of Harrington's presence at a spring 1989 conference at Barnard College, his easy manner of association with and obvious respect for issues important to young people. His responsive presence was evident in conversations with students on numerous occasions over the years.

Because of the catholicity of Harrington's interests and the qualities of his mind, almost anyone committed to the struggle for justice and peace was likely to regard him as an ally. In addition to the works analyzing capitalism's disenfranchisement of the poor, he was sensitive, also, to the collapse of Western culture reflected in the arts, philosophy, and religion. This theme informs *The Accidental Century* (1965) and *The Politics at God's Funeral: The Spiritual Crisis of Western Civilization* (1983), particularly. "The accidental revolution has resulted, not in this or that loss of faith, but in introducing doubt and contradiction into every Western creed, secular or religious," he argued in the first book, a condition explored again with remarkable insight and sympathy in the second book. Because of his sensitivity to art as well as his knowledge of the social sciences, almost everything Harrington wrote deserves a reading; and fortunately several of his books remain in print.

BY MICHAEL HARRINGTON
The Accidental Century. New York: Macmillan, 1962, 1969.

Fragments of the Century: A Social Autobiography. New York: E. P. Dutton, 1973.

The Long-Distance Runner: An Autobiography. New York: Henry Holt and Co., 1988.

The Other America: Poverty in America. New York: Macmillan, 1963.

The Politics at God's Funeral: The Spiritual Crisis of Western Civilization. New York: Holt, Rinehart and Winston, 1983.

The Vast Majority: A Journey to the World's Poor. New York: Simon and Schuster, 1977.

Socialism. New York: Saturday Review Press, 1972.

DENISE LEVERTOV
1923-

IN "MAKING PEACE," A VOICE CRIES OUT FROM THE DARK,
saying that poets must give us peace "to oust the intense, familiar
imagination of disaster." Responding to that challenge, the principal speaker in the poem answers,

> But peace, like a poem,
> is not there ahead of itself...
> can't be known except
> in the words of its making,
> grammar of justice,
> syntax of mutual aid.

Building a new social order and making a new language are parallel activities, calling for a restructuring of life and idiom:

a line of peace might appear
if we restructured the sentence our lives are making,
revoked its reaffirmation of profit and power,
questioned our need, allowed
long pauses...

In life, as in art, Levertov's poem suggests, the time has come for a revaluation of values. On that condition rests our hope for appropriate language, to sustain us, and for a new social order.

Some years before Levertov wrote "Making Peace," hundreds of distinguished American artists had endeavored, individually and collectively, to "make peace" by supporting the anti-war effort. From its initiation in 1965 by Robert Bly and David Ray, Poets Against the War in Vietnam sponsored benefit readings and public forums on campuses and in communities and helped to clarify the moral and political issues associated with U.S. intervention. In June, the same year, Robert Lowell, perhaps the most "public" poet of his generation, turned down President Lyndon Johnson's invitation to a White House Festival of the Arts because of Johnson's war. In a carefully written, even courteous letter, Lowell warned that the administration's policy toward Vietnam put the U.S. "in danger of imperceptibly becoming an explosive and suddenly chauvinistic nation." Other writers, including Stanley Kunitz, Bernard Malamud, Mary McCarthy, and Dwight McDonald, supporting Lowell's decision, expressed "dismay at recent American foreign policy decisions."

Other artists described the agony and suffering inflicted by military forces on both sides, and in *Armies of the Night: The Novel as History, the History as Novel* (1968), Norman Mailer gave a moving, autobiographical narrative about the 1967 March on the Pentagon, which brought a hundred thousand people to a major demonstration in Washington. Well-known poets took political risks in addressing moral questions associated with American policy by writing poems of remarkable artistic skill and integrity and by committing acts of civil disobedience against the war and the draft. In 1968, at a ceremony in New York City, as Vice President Hubert Humphrey looked on, Robert Bly gave the $1,000 check accompanying his National Book Award for *The Light Around the Body* (1967) to a young draft resister, Michael Kempton. Similarly, Muriel Rukeyser endured arrest in anti-draft demonstrations, and Allen Ginsberg, echoing Henry David Thoreau's "Civil Disobedience," encouraged citizens to refuse to pay taxes supporting war.

Among the many lyric poems that took the Vietnam war as a theme, Robert Bly's "Asian Peace Offers Rejected Without Publication" conveys the despair that many Americans felt as the troop shipments increased from fifty thousand to two-hundred-fifty thousand to five-hundred thousand American troops and as negotiations for a cease-fire failed again and again. As Bly suggests in this eloquent poem, neither presidents nor advisers had any intention of ending the war:

These suggestions by Asians are not taken seriously.
We know Rusk smiles as he passes them to someone.
Men like Rusk are not men only—
They are bombs waiting to be loaded in a darkened hangar.
Rusk's assistants eat hurriedly,
Talking of Teilhard de Chardin,
Longing to get back to their offices
So they can cling to the underside of the steel wings
shuddering faintly in the high altitudes.

Other poems of similar skill that took the war as their theme include Robert Bly's long poem, *The Teeth Mother Naked at Last* (1970); and lyrics such as David Ignatow's "All Quiet—Written at the start of one of our bombing pauses over North Vietnam"; Muriel Rukeyser's "Poem," beginning "I lived in the first century of world war"; Allen Ginsberg's "Wichita Vortex Sutra"; Levertov's remarkable collection *The Sorrow Dance* (1967); and other poems based upon actual experience in Vietnam.

Levertov publicly opposed the war long before 1968, when her husband, Mitchell Goodman, was indicted with Dr. Benjamin Spock, Michael Ferber, and others, in the first "conspiracy" trial initiated by the U.S. government. The government's various attempts to undermine and to discredit the anti-war movement failed; in addition, activists and writers, in their trials, informed the general public about real, rather than superficial, consequences of that war "reported" in the popular media.

Born October 24, 1923, in Ilford, Essex, England, Denise Levertov moved to the U.S. in 1947 and became a citizen in 1955. The daughter of an Anglican clergyman—a convert from Hasidic Judaism, and of a Welsh descendant of the prophet Angel Jones, Levertov published her first collection of poems, *The Double Image*, in 1946, since followed by over forty books of poetry, prose, and translation. Recognized as a major poet of the Post-modernist period, she has taught at colleges and universities throughout the country—including, at present, Stanford University—and has received numerous awards and honorary degrees in recognition of her achievement.

Long resident in New England, Levertov lives now in Seattle, gives frequent public readings, and publishes new collections of poetry and prose. Recent longer works include "Mass for the Feast of St. Thomas Didymus" and "El Salvador—Requiem and Invocation," an oratorio set to music, about the U.S.-financed war against the poor in that Central American country. In her own life and writing, Denise Levertov maintains an active commitment to justice and peace organizations, which she supports with frequent benefit readings.

A persistent theme in Levertov's prose and poetry is the artist's place in society and the individual's responsibilities for the common good. As with other contemporary artists, Levertov has decried the effect of Cold War rhetoric, its poisoning of the moral atmosphere. Through her poems, a reader senses the grief, fury, and despair that has accompanied this corruption of language. In emphasizing the need for a revitalization of language as a requirement for social change, Levertov agrees with Virginia Woolf's statement, in another context: "My sympathies were all on the side of life." And Levertov's poetry is a powerful source of inspiration and encouragement for "constructing peace" in a violent era.

In a large body of work, Levertov's "Life at War " from *The Sor-*

row Dance (1967) and "Making Peace" from *Breathing the Water* (1984) are particularly concerned with the effects of war and violence on contemporary culture. Both poems bring together personal and social concerns—private life and public issues—that have haunted writers particularly since 1914.

The initial reference point in "Life at War" is a statement by Rainer Maria Rilke during the First World War, followed by a lament that "the same war continues." The speaker describes our loss of hope at a time when our memories, even the membranes of our bodies, carry remnants of perpetual war:

We have breathed the grits of it in, all our lives
our lungs are pocked with it,
the mucous membrane of our dreams
coated with it, the imagination
filmed over with the gray filth of it.

In direct conflict with this knowledge is the poet's awareness of another humankind, "whose flesh responds to a caress, whose eyes/ are flowers that perceive the stars,/ whose music excels the music of birds." Which of these definitions of humankind will prevail, the poem asks? Which language will we choose to speak?

In the years since she wrote that poem, Levertov has struggled to find appropriate responses to these questions. Endeavoring to keep things whole, she has refused to surrender to that dissociation of sensibility that separates the individual person from the common life of all.

"O, language, mother of thought," she asked in *Staying Alive,* "are you rejecting us as we reject you?" George Orwell posed that question initially, just after the Second World War, as have writers of the Post-modernist period in confronting lies and violence justified by "politics and the English language" over the past fifty years.

Through "a religious devotion to the truth, to the splendor of the authentic," as Levertov once put it, she has named and confronted these injustices, imagined a better future, and occasionally given it exotic form in poetry. A vision of that possible future, arising out of contemplation and action, is evoked in "Making

Peace," quoted above, and in another recent poem, "About Political Action in Which Each Individual Acts from the Heart":

> When solitaries draw close, releasing
> each solitude into its blossoming,
>
> when we give to each other the roses
> of our communion—
>
> a culture of gardens, horticulture not agribusiness,
> arbors among the lettuce, small terrains—
>
> when we taste in small victories sometimes
> the small, ephemeral yet joyful
> harvest of our striving,
>
> great power flows from us,
> luminous, a promise. Yes! . . . Then
> great energy flows from solitude,
> and great power from communion.

BY DENISE LEVERTOV
Breathing the Water. New York: New Directions, 1988.

Candles in Babylon. New York: New Directions, 1982.

The Poet in the World. New York: New Directions, 1973.

The Sorrow Dance. New York: New Directions, 1967.

ABOUT DENISE LEVERTOV
A Poetry Reading Against the Vietnam War. Robert Bly and David Ray, eds. Madison, Minn.: The Sixties Press, 1966.

Breslin, James E. B. *From Modern to Contempoary American Poetry 1945-1965.* Chicago: University of Chicago Press, 1984.

Mersmann, James F. *Out of the Vietnam Vortex: A Study of Poets and Poetry Against the War.* Lawrence: University Press of Kansas, 1974.

Poetry and Politics: An Anthology of Essays. Richard Jones, ed. New York: Quill, 1985.

Wagner, Linda W. *Denise Levertov.* New York: Twayne, 1967.

Raymond Hunthausen
1921-

WAS IT THE GROWING NUMBER OF CATHOLIC PRELATES protesting nuclear weapons that led to the Vatican's disciplining of Archbishop Hunthausen in 1986? And why did the Roman hierarchy choose to embarrass a popular leader by limiting the power of his office in such a public way? Or did the Roman Curia simply agree with conservative Catholics and the arms lobby in the Seattle area who wrote to Rome to "tattle" on Hunthausen? Also, how closely did the Vatican work with the F.B.I. and C.I.A. in silencing this critic of U.S. nuclear policy? Citizens concerned about public debate and religious liberty in the U.S. may wonder about this now, just as they did at the time of Rome's intervention.

When, in 1982, short, stocky "Dutch" Hunthausen announced that he was refusing to pay part of his income tax as a protest against nuclear weapons, few people followed suit. Even as archbishop of a large diocese, he commanded few legions; and in truth, he was not the first man in such a visible, prestigious office to disobey the law for conscience's sake. Before him, Bishops Thomas Gumbleton of Detroit, "a total pacifist," and Charles Buswell of Pueblo, Colorado, had publicly protested U.S. policy in Vietnam and the nuclear arms buildup. Influenced by the writings of Dorothy Day, Thomas Merton, and Gordon Zahn, they were joined by other bishops, including the late Carroll Dozier of Memphis, Leroy Matthiesen of Amarillo, and Walter Sullivan of Richmond, Virginia. Since the early 1970s, 100 bishops in all have joined Pax Christi, with several being arrested for civil disobedience at nuclear testing sites or nuclear arms depots.

Hunthausen had first suggested withholding tax payments to the "nuclear-armed Caesar" at a Lutheran conference in the summer of 1981. Shortly thereafter, during their annual meeting in Washington, D.C., John Roach of St. Paul, president of 300 American Catholic bishops, called upon his colleagues to help stop the arms race. On a global scale, he said, it is "the most dangerous moral issue in the public order today," and the church "needs to say 'no' clearly and decisively to the use of nuclear arms." Could any moral person disagree?

Statements resembling Archbishop Roach's and the subsequent bishops' pastoral, *The Challenge of Peace: God's Promise and Our Response* (1983), raised anxieties among people bound by dominant Cold War myths and policies. Some Catholics even resented religious leaders' complaints about the arms race taking money, talent, and energy from the public till (with an attendant lack of resources for human services). Under Reagan, who regarded Russia as "the evil empire," bishops were vulnerable to attack from right-wing communicants on "doctrinal" grounds as well. Some Catholics, for example, criticized Hunthausen for being tolerant of gays and lesbians and for allowing non-Catholics to participate fully in religious celebrations.

Meanwhile, voters and politicians, under the sway of the dominant rhetoric, undid social programs in place since the 1930s. Many lawmakers and readers of *The Wanderer*, a Catholic periodical known for its conservative views, expected clergy to remain quiescent or unconcerned about political matters relating to foreign policy particularly. In that atmosphere, a conventionally religious and decent man who lived his values—as Hunthausen does—was regarded as "outrageous." Eventually letter writers from Hunthausen's diocese and Vatican hard-liners, under the influence of Cardinal Ratzinger and probably with information supplied by the F.B.I., succeeded in undermining Hunthausen's leadership.

Born August 2, 1921, in Anaconda, Montana, a town named for the copper company that once dominated that mining area, Raymond G. Hunthausen is the oldest of seven children. As a boy, he worked in his father's grocery store while attending the parochial grammar school. There he became known for his intelligence and effective, if reluctant, leadership among the students. At Carroll College, a small, local Catholic institution, he majored in chemistry; but rather than becoming an air force fighter pilot, as he planned, he took the suggestion of his math teacher, a priest, who encouraged him to study for the seminary. Although horrified by the U.S. decision to drop the bomb on Japan without warning in 1945, while he was studying for the priesthood, Hunthausen "lived with this reality just like the rest of the world [but] didn't do anything about it."

Ordained in 1948, he studied at Notre Dame University and completed an LL. D. degree at DePaul University, Chicago. After teaching chemistry, and coaching football and basketball at his undergraduate college, he served as its president from 1957 to 1962. That year, when John XXIII convened the Second Vatican Council, Hunthausen was named Bishop of Helena, Montana; in 1975, under Paul VI, he became Archbishop of Seattle. Although he had signed statements protesting the deployment of nuclear missiles in Montana, it was a meeting with Jim Douglass, a long-time anti-nuclear activist at the Trident submarine base, that turned Hunthausen toward nonviolent resistance. A former teacher in Notre Dame University's short-lived program in nonviolence and author of *The Non-Violent Cross* (1968), Jim, with Shelly Douglass, lived in voluntary poverty. Impressed by Douglass' faith and effort, Hunthausen wrote to priests in his diocese, citing an article by Richard McSorley, S.J., about the taproot of violence being people's willingness to live with nuclear destruction.

After taking that initiative, Hunthausen spoke publicly, even willingly, and was invited to several parishes, particularly those near the military base. "I said yes to one parish council and discovered when I arrived that the hall was filled," he wrote in 1983. Later, invited by a Lutheran bishop, who had been withholding his war taxes for some time, to speak at a synod in Tacoma, Washington, Hunthausen indicated that he supported tax resistance and generally endorsed unilateral disarmament, for "when crimes are being prepared in our name, we must speak plainly. I saw with a deep consciousness of these words that Trident is the Auschwitz of Puget Sound."

At the Bangor, Washington, naval base, Hunthausen participated in protests organized by the Pacific Life Community and the Ground Zero community. Eventually, Bishop Larry Matthiesen became involved in nuclear protests at the Pantex Corporation, Amarillo, Texas, bombmakers at the other end of the line. With Hunthausen's support, the protests organized by Jim and Shelley Douglass and others at the nuclear submarine base flourished, and exposed the dangers of nuclear power among workers and the general populace.

In the midst of this activity, however, the Vatican began a series of investigative procedures against and visitations to Hunthausen that can only be described as Byzantine or simply bizarre. Archbishop James Hickey of Washington, D.C., the Vatican representative, conducted taped interviews with Hunthausen and his staff, lay and religious leaders, including outspoken critics accusing Hunthausen of "open disobedience of the Holy Father on matters of faith and morals." And although 90 percent of the priests in the archdiocese signed a petition supporting Hunthausen, his authority was called into question, and an assistant appointed, without prior consultation. After dragging on for a year, the investigation ended, however, with all of Hunthausen's powers of office restored.

In an interview prior to the Vatican's investigation, Hunthausen responded to a question about the likelihood of "the ruling power" turning against the church if it were identified with the poor and with peace. He would find it hard, he said in the 1981 interview, to accept the victimization by "the ruling power" of "a peace church or a church for the poor." If the church opposes the interests of those in power, he acknowledged, however, "we have to expect to suffer some kind of retaliation." And in the case of his "peace church" of the Upper Pacific Northwest, church and state cooperated to retaliate against him.

Although his response to the investigation was characteristically measured, tolerant, even conciliatory, Hunthausen kept on with the nuclear protests and public responses to actions against him. His integrity as an administrator is suggested by a tribute from George Weigel, who disagrees pointedly with Hunthausen's "nonviolence." As publisher of the diocesan newspaper, Hunthausen allowed Weigel "an unfettered critical voice" in his column opposing Hunthausen. "I can imagine few other dioceses in the United States where this situation would have obtained," Weigel added.

In a very real way, Hunthausen not only survived the ordeal of the investigation; he triumphed. Enduring a bout with cancer and other complicating factors, he eventually enjoyed the return of his powers of office and saw the growth of the anti-nuclear movement. Now retired as archbishop, he limits activities principally to his home area, while supporting the peace movement in the modest and pastoral manner that has characterized his administration and ministry from the beginning.

BY RAYMOND HUNTHAUSEN
Introduction to William Treacy, *Biblical Meditations on Peace.* Kansas City: Sheed and Ward, 1985.

ABOUT RAYMOND HUNTHAUSEN
Gumbleton, Thomas, Raymond Hunthausen, Leroy Matthiesen, and Walter Sullivan: "Four Bishops," in *Peace Makers: Christian*

Voices From the New Abolitionist Movement. Jim Wallis, ed. San Francisco: Harper & Row, 1983.

Lernoux, Penny. *People of God: The Struggle for World Catholicism.* New York: Viking Press, 1989.

Weigel, George. *Tranquillitas Ordinis: The Present Failure and Future Promise of American Catholic Thought on War and Peace.* New York: Oxford University Press, 1987.

ELISE BOULDING
1910-
and
KENNETH BOULDING
1920-

ELISE BOULDING HAS DESCRIBED THE MODEST BEGIN-
nings of the International Peace Research Association (IPRA) in
1965 as "a small group of participants from different continents
talking about how they could support one another in turning
their scientific knowledge to the elimination of war." With her
husband, Kenneth Boulding, and others providing a theoretical
base, scholars from Europe, Asia, Africa, and the Americas

gradually aligned their efforts for "positive peace" with their vocations as teachers and researchers.

Kenneth and Elise Boulding met in the spring of 1941 at a gathering where she was "taken into membership by the Society of Friends (Quakers)," she wrote forty-eight years later. In the meantime, their achievement in writing, teaching, and organizing has led to Nobel prize nominations, he in economics and she for peace. By their activism and their scholarship, as co-founders of IPRA, which she has served as executive secretary, and its North American affiliate, the Consortium on Peace Research, Education and Development (COPRED), the couple has influenced the lives of many people, especially teachers and researchers in peace and world security studies.

Born in Oslo, July 6, 1920, Elise Bjorn-Hansen moved to the United States as a young woman, graduated from Douglass College, and in 1941 married Kenneth Boulding. Though a committed pacifist, she looked to Kenneth, ten years older, "as teacher/ companion/guide" in peacemaking. While rearing five children and becoming involved in movements for social change ("I began working for peace there, in the context of family and community."), she completed graduate study at Iowa State University and the University of Michigan, wrote for professional journals, and served as director of several organizations associated with peace studies and women's studies. As a sociologist, she taught at the University of Colorado, Boulder, then later at Dartmouth College. "The scholar-activist dichotomy has never been an issue for me," she has said. "There is nothing without practice, and data is useless without experientially grounded models that can show how facts interrelate."

Integrating means and ends, in working for peace, has been a preoccupation of Elise Boulding since the beginning. "The way we work is as important as the issues on which we work," she told the vice president of Pax Christi International. "Each of us must choose a focus, but unless we keep in mind the connections, our work loses its relevance." Influenced by Fred Polac, a Dutch author whose book she translated, she agrees with him that society moves toward "the future it envisions."

Kenneth Boulding's major contribution to peace research is at once subtle and deep, reflecting the wide intellectual interests and competencies of the man. Uncompromising in his commitment to peace, he recognized, nonetheless, the deficiency in its social theory, which led to "frequent breakdowns" interrupting the progress of the movement. Much of his scholarly writing arose from a conviction "that the intellectual chassis of the broad movement for the abolition of war has not been adequate to support the powerful moral engine which drives it." For that reason particularly, he has worked to improve the theoretical and intellectual underpinnings of structures for peace. His *Stable Peace* (1978), based upon lectures at the University of Texas, is perhaps his most skillful, readable reflection on the nature of such structures.

Economist, teacher, author, and pacifist, Kenneth Ewart Boulding is a native of Liverpool, England, where he was born January 18, 1910. Reared a Methodist, he found in the Quaker meeting in Liverpool, and later at Oxford, a place where religious experience complemented "his deepening intellectual grasp of the world." Planning to study chemistry, he eventually settled on economics, and after completing undergraduate and graduate degrees at Oxford University, received a faculty appointment at the University of Edinburgh, Scotland. Invited to teach at Colgate University during a visit to the United States in 1937, he has since taught at many universities in this country and abroad, for a number of years at the University of Michigan and the University of Colorado, Boulder, as professor emeritus since 1980.

Along the way, living his pacifist principles got Boulding into trouble. In 1942, for example, he lost a job as a staff member with the League of Nations Economic and Financial Section, in New Jersey, for circulating a statement asking people to give up their national allegiances and to cast away their weapons. In 1948, he waged a legal battle to become a naturalized U.S. citizen without taking the oath to bear arms. An activist/academic, he initiated campaigns against nuclear testing and the draft, refused to sign stringent loyalty oaths during the McCarthy era, and supported movements for social change in body as well as in principle. All of these tasks were accomplished, his associates say, with good humor and with time for writing sonnets that mark the principal occasions of his life.

The inspiration for and the origins of Elise and Kenneth Boulding's combined effort for peace were his passionate conviction as a youth "that war was the major moral and intellectual problem of our age"; and her realization in 1940, when Hitler invaded Norway, her native country, "that the only way to have security is to have it for everyone." An early cooperative venture was the Center for Conflict Resolution at the University of Michigan, which Kenneth helped to initiate and Elise served as volunteer secretary/editor/networker in the late 1950s and early 1960s. About the same time, Students for a Democratic Society, involving some of their Michigan students, issued the Port Huron Statement, followed soon afterward by the first teach-ins against the Vietnam war.

In post–World War Two America, when universities were often co-opted by the war-making state in the service of the C.I.A. or the Pentagon, Kenneth Boulding's priorities were ignored by most academics. Cold War rhetoric, in its attempts "to make lies sound truthful and murder respectable and to give the appearance of solidity to pure wind," as Orwell said in 1947, left little room for talk of peace research, as many scholars enlisted in—or tolerated the inanities of—the military-industrial-university complex.

In his manner of conducting himself, as citizen and scholar, Boulding offered an alternative to academic Cold Warriors embracing the politics of the moment. Long before university presidents from around the world spoke, in their 1989 Talloires Declaration, of the need for "language, history, culture, and methods to create peace," and before the American bishops, in their 1983 pastoral letter, urged Catholic universities "to develop programs for rigorous, interdisciplinary research, education and training directed toward peacemaking expertise," Boulding had begun that painstaking, moral, and intellectual effort.

The Bouldings' active involvement in the issues of their time helped to keep the new discipline of peace studies from becoming just another trendy discipline, "merely academic." "Despairing of protest, others have turned toward violence, but he has turned toward knowledge," Cynthia Kerman, Kenneth's biographer, says. And the Bouldings' projects and publications—poetry, religious reflections, economic and sociological treatises—have earned them public recognition, including many honorary degrees and reputations as two of the essential social scientists of our time.

By the early 1970s, the Bouldings were cooperating with other scholars committed to "education for an interdependent world": Chadwick Alger at Ohio State University; Bernice Carroll at the University of Illinois; Betty Reardon at Columbia University, for example, and Anatol Rapoport, Canada; Johan Galtung, Norway; and Yoshikazu Sakamoto, Japan. As peace researchers, they recognized the various instabilities "resulting from the Cold War era and the failure of Western-based development strategies," as Elise Boulding told the twenty-fifth annual IPRA conference in Groningen, the Netherlands, in 1990. Since 1965, participation at such meetings, on weapons technology, human rights, nonviolence, and ecology, had increased from 71 people from 22 countries, to 341 people from 57 countries, in an organization numbering 1000 members.

In a verse-prophecy—one of many good-natured poetic responses to changing times, Kenneth Boulding once described IPRA and COPRED as attempts to integrate

Research and Training, in one wise
And fruitful kind of enterprise.

In the 1990s, these goals inform a number of graduate and undergraduate programs in peace studies and conflict resolution—at Syracuse, George Mason, and Notre Dame universities, for example, and in publicly funded, state-wide programs in Ohio and New York. "COPRED cannot claim all the credit,/But still it made more plus than debit," Boulding rightly observed, while emphasizing the hard "peacework" remaining to be done:

And if we don't get up and do it,
Somebody's surely going to rue it.
And things may go from bad to worse,
Like this incessant doggerel verse.

BY KENNETH AND ELISE BOULDING

Boulding, Elise, *Building a Global Civil Culture: Education for an Interdependent World*. Syracuse: Syracuse University Press, 1990.

_____. *One Small Plot of Heaven: Reflections on Family Life by a Quaker Sociologist*. Wallingford, Penn.: Pendle Hill Publications, 1989.

Boulding, Kenneth. *Sonnets from the Interior Life and Other Biographical Verse*. Boulder, Col.: Colorado Associated University Press, 1975.

_____. *Stable Peace*. Austin: University of Texas Press, 1976.

ABOUT KENNETH AND ELISE BOULDING

"Imaging a World at Peace": Interview with Elise Boulding. *Pax Christi USA*, Spring 1988, 18-19.

Kerman, Cynthia. *Creative Tension: The Life and Thought of Kenneth Boulding*. Ann Arbor: University of Michigan Press, 1974.

Frontiers in Social Thought: Essays in Honor of Kenneth E. Boulding. Martin Pfaff, ed. North-Holland, 1976.

Oscar Romero
1917-1980

ROMERO, PERHAPS THE MOST POWERFUL RELIGIOUS FILM
I have ever seen, introduced many people in the United States to
the life of Oscar Romero, and suggested why his example informs
the hearts and minds of millions, particularly in Latin America
and the Third World. In less than a decade, he has joined the company of Gandhi and Martin Luther King as an inspiration and
guide in the struggle for human rights and nonviolent social
change. Some people think that in time he will be canonized.

When he was consecrated archbishop of San Salvador in 1977, Oscar Romero appeared a safe choice—timid, scholarly, "spiritual." Moderate in his opinions and critical of liberation theologians, Romero was regarded as "a compromise candidate" among the native clergy, someone who would neither challenge nor upset the ruling oligarchy of El Salvador. In this smallest, most densely populated country of Central America—on the Pacific Ocean, between Guatemala and Honduras—the rich owned 80 percent of the land, and the army, with U.S. military equipment and training, enforced the status quo by terrorizing workers and landless peasants.

In his first letter to fellow clergy, shortly after festivities marking his consecration, Romero spoke in traditional—abstract, though hardly platitudinous—language about a religious faith "that identifies us with the one priesthood of Christ...and all the human virtues that nourish our supernatural communion on the natural and psychological levels."

Three years later, when he lay dead in a convent chapel, after being shot while saying Mass, people looked back at that earlier letter. Jon Sobrino, a Jesuit theologian in Romero's diocese who had had reservations about his appointment as archbishop, reflected on the younger Romero: "His theology was questionable. Beyond question, however, was his profound faith in God, and his surpassing concern for the glory of God in this world." In the intervening years, Oscar Romero's perspective on what constituted "the glory of God in this world" had changed. Some called that change "a conversion"; others regarded it as a natural consequence of his concern for and dedication to his people in a dangerous time.

Whatever the reasons for it, his altered perspective had profound implications for the church in El Salvador and the response of the ruling oligarchy toward that institution. In a speech that Romero gave one month before he was murdered, he described the profound implications of his change for the poor, for theology, for the church (the translation is Philip Berryman's):

We believe in Jesus
who came to give life in abundance

and we believe in a living God
who gives life to human beings
and wants them to truly live.
These radical truths of faith
become real truths...
when the church involves itself
in the life and death of its people.
So the church,
like every person,
is faced with the most basic option for its faith,
being for life or death....
on this point there is no possible neutrality.
We either serve the life of Salvadorans
or we are accomplices in their death....
We either believe in a God of life
or we serve the idols of death.

Re-reading Romero's words during this tense period and knowing the price he paid for uttering them make one wonder at the courage that sustained him.

Born August 15, 1917, in eastern El Salvador, near the Honduran border, Oscar Arnulfo Romero was the second child of Santos Romero and Guadalupe de Jesus Galdamez. Leaving home at thirteen, where he worked as a carpenter's apprentice, he made a seven-hour trip by horseback in order to enter the minor seminary at San Miguel. At twenty, he transferred to the national seminary in San Salvador before being sent to Rome, where he was ordained a priest in 1942.

Returning to his own diocese in El Salvador for the next twenty-five years, Romero gained a reputation as a kind but demanding priest. In 1967, he was transferred to the capital city of San Salvador, and later, as auxiliary bishop, was assigned to secondary tasks. Generally sympathetic, like many Latin American bishops, to the historic realignment of the Catholic church toward the poor after the Second Vatican Council, Romero was nonetheless close to priests associated with Opus Dei and critical of liberation theology.

As bishop of his old diocese in the early 1970s, according to one of his priests, Romero quoted documents of the Second Vatican

Council; but he never referred to those of Medellin, by Latin American bishops. In 1977, although many clergy probably preferred his contemporary Arturo Rivera Damas, Romero was named successor to Archbishop Luis Chavez y Gonzalez, who had sided with working people in their efforts for better wages and working conditions.

Speaking always for peaceful reform, Romero soon had to face the fact, as a national leader, that the government made no distinction between people working for nonviolent social change and those advocating violent revolution. In the eyes of state officials, everyone for reform was "a doctrinaire Marxist," including nuns and priests teaching in Catholic schools; and uniformed soldiers or secret death squads killed increasing numbers of human-rights activists, students, and technicians, as well as urban guerillas armed against the oligarchy.

Only weeks after his consecration as archbishop, Romero had to officiate at the funeral of Father Rutilio Grande, a personal friend and master of ceremonies at Romero's episcopal ordination. A popular priest, whose sermons denounced the exploitation of the many by the few, Rutilio, along with a young boy and an old man, was murdered as he drove a jeep across the flat sugarcane fields, one of the few places landless campesinos could find work in his region.

Not long afterward, Romero began to speak more directly about the suffering of his people and the proper response of Christians to that condition. "A church that does not unite itself to the poor in order to denounce from the place of the poor the injustice committed against them is not truly the Church of Jesus Christ," he said. For Romero, the place of the poor in El Salvador became indistinguishable from "the place of the skull," where Christ died, and he increasingly identified their suffering with the suffering of Jesus. In Sunday sermons, from the Cathedral in El Salvador, he demanded an accounting of the abuses by the police and an end to the war between the national army and guerillas. And when El Salvador's president offered him protection, Romero, though fearing his own death, answered that rather than his own security, what he wanted was "security and tranquility for 108 families and their 'disappeared,'" adding that a "shepherd seeks no security as long as the flock is threatened."

In a letter to Jimmy Carter, six weeks before Romero's death, he expressed hope that the president's religious sentiments and sensitivity to human rights would move him to halt U.S. economic and military assistance to the military junta, "thus avoiding greater bloodshed in this suffering country." And on March 23, 1980, the day before Romero was murdered, he spoke directly to those primarily responsible for the violence, those under government orders:

> We are your people. The peasants you kill are your own brothers and sisters. When you hear the voice of the man commanding you to kill, remember instead the voice of God. Thou Shalt Not Kill....No soldier is obliged to obey an order contrary to the law of God. There is still time for you to obey your conscience, even in the face of a sinful command to kill.
>
> The church, defender of the rights of God, of the law of God, and the dignity of each human being, cannot remain silent in the presence of such abominations. In the name of God, in the name of our tormented people whose cries rise up to Heaven, I beseech you, I beg you, I command you, *stop the repression.*

Over a decade after his death, Romero's spirit is more alive than ever among those working at home and abroad to alleviate the violence, including ending U.S. military intervention in Central America. Ignoring Romero, the Carter administration—but more cynically, the Reagan and Bush administrations—made every citizen of the U.S. complicit in the deaths of seventy thousand people in El Salvador. Those murdered included citizens of the U.S., such as Sisters Maura Clarke, M.M., Ita Ford, M.M., Dorothy Kazel, O.S.U., and Jean Donovan, who were murdered eight months after Romero. Not until six Jesuit priests and two women were murdered, similarly, in 1989 did the U.S. government seriously reconsider its massive aid to the Salvadoran military, then second only to U.S. aid to Israel.

"The word remains. This is the great comfort of one who preaches," Romero had said in a 1978 homily. "My voice will disappear, but my word, which is Christ, will remain." At the end of a murderous decade, whatever peace comes to El Salvador and whatever hope landless, impoverished peasants enjoy owes a debt to the theology of Oscar Romero and to the ultimate sacrifice that it required of him.

BY OSCAR ROMERO
Voice of the Voiceless: The Four Pastoral Letters and Other Statements. Maryknoll, N.Y.: Orbis Books, 1985.

ABOUT OSCAR ROMERO
Berryman, Phillip. *The Religious Roots of Rebellion: Christians in Central American Revolutions.* Maryknoll, N.Y.: Orbis Books, 1984.

Brockman, James R., S.J. *The Word Remains: A Life of Oscar Romero.* Maryknoll, N.Y.: Orbis Books, 1982.

Sobrino, Jon. *Archbishop Romero: Memories and Reflections.* Robert R. Barr, transl. Maryknoll, N.Y.: Orbis Books, 1990.

THOMAS MERTON
1915-1968

ALTHOUGH HE LIVED MUCH OF HIS ADULT LIFE CLOIS-
tered as a Trappist monk, Thomas Merton was partly responsible
for the emergence of an active community for nonviolent social
change among American Catholics; he prodded, even provoked
them out of a kind of social torpor. Before the mid-sixties, few
American Catholics were visible in movements initiated and sustained by civil rights and pacifist groups—the National Association for the Advancement of Colored People (NAACP), for example, or historic peace churches or organizations.

Through the influence of Dorothy Day and the Catholic Worker movement and the writings of Merton and Gordon Zahn, American Catholics began to join and eventually to initiate activist groups addressing a range of issues related to civil rights and nuclear disarmament. By 1970, they were visible as "the Catholic conspiracy against the war," as Zahn called it, and formidable enough to provoke the ire of fellow communicant J. Edgar Hoover, the politically powerful head of the Federal Bureau of Investigation. Other important contributors to a change in attitude among American Catholics were the Second Vatican Council (1962-65); John XXIII, its initiator; and his encyclicals *Mater et Magistra* and *Pacem in Terris*. Traditionally working class—as well as liberal and Democratic in their voting record since 1928—Catholics had seldom been central to movements for fundamental social change and never at the center of a peace movement. After 1964, in part because of Thomas Merton, first individual members, then the institutional church, began to change.

The year 1964 is a key time for new currents in Catholic social thought because of several events, including (1) the publication of Gordon Zahn's *In Solitary Witness: The Life and Death of Franz Jagerstatter*, following his important book *German Catholics and Hitler's Wars* two years earlier; (2) the founding of the Catholic Peace Fellowship; and (3) a retreat on the "Spiritual Roots of Protest" at the Cistercian (Trappist) Abbey of Our Lady of Gethsemani, Kentucky.

1. John XXIII's encyclical evoked support for a peace movement, beginning with a major U.N.-related conference sponsored by the Center for the Study of Democratic Institutions and involving Robert Hutchins, John Cogley, and a host of internationally known scholars, editors, and political leaders. Similarly, Zahn's biography of Jagerstatter provided a powerful example of a devout Austrian peasant who, like many young Catholic conscientious objectors later on, simply said "No!" to killing—in his case, as a potential member of Hitler's army.

2. Catholic Peace Fellowship, a branch of the Fellowship of Reconciliation, was initiated by Tom Cornell and James Forest, former editors of the *Catholic Worker*, and Philip Berrigan, a Josephite priest at that time.

3. The Trappist retreat, involving Cornell, Forest, Berrigan, and others, included presentations by A. J. Muste, John Howard Yoder, Daniel Berrigan, S.J., and most significantly, Thomas Merton, on "The Monastic Protest: The Voice in the Wilderness." Four years later, several participants were in prison for burning draft files at selective service offices throughout the U.S.

In published notes for "Spiritual Roots of Protest," Merton expressed hope of finding "common grounds for *religious dissent and commitment* in the face of the injustice and disorder of a world in which total war seems at times inevitable...." He sought "not the formulation of a program, but a deepening of roots," when others appeared to be offering only "violent solutions to economic and social problems more critical and more vast than man has ever known before." From his notes, it is clear that Merton had been thinking about, had even been haunted by, these concerns for some time. As recently as 1962, he had joined PAX, a U.S. branch of a British peace organization, had written for and corresponded frequently with editors of the *Catholic Worker*, and had edited an important anthology, *Breakthrough to Peace*, for New Directions; it included essays by others concerned about the nuclear arms race: Erich Fromm, Lewis Mumford, Norman Cousins, and Gordon Zahn.

Merton's introduction to *Breakthrough to Peace* surveys in a prophetic way the complex moral and spiritual questions that have occupied scientists, ethicists, artists, and theologians ever since. It addresses directly, for example, what Robert Jay Lifton later called "psychic numbing" and what Merton regarded as "secret forces that rise up within us and dictate fatal decisions." Such behavior can only be countered by a morality, a wisdom that permeates "every judgment, every choice, every political act that deserves to be called civilized." To act in that way, Merton added, we must

shake off our passive irresponsibility, renounce our
fatalistic submission to economic and social forces,
and give up the unquestioning belief in machines and
processes which characterizes the mass mind.

Four years later, in 1968, the year that Merton died in Bangkok, he wrote another essay that develops a similar theme, with particular reference to the Cold War's corruption of language. As a writer, Merton was angry, as Orwell had been in "Politics and the English Language" (1946), about those who Orwell said try "to make lies sound truthful and murder respectable, and to give the appearance of solidity to pure wind." Merton focused on a warrior "language" used to accomplish similar goals: "the pompous and sinister jargon of the war mandarins in government offices and military think-tanks." Generally, Merton's "War and the Crisis of Language" brings together themes informing his other perceptive writings on peace; it also fleshes out his discussion of approaches to social change in an earlier pamphlet, "Blessed Are the Meek: The Christian Roots of Nonviolence." A lifetime of experience, writing, and reflection had brought him to this point. For that reason, among others, the posthumously published volume *Thomas Merton on Peace* (or *The Nonviolent Alternative*), with Gordon Zahn's introduction, occupies a special place among classic statements on nonviolence.

Born January 31, 1915, in Prades, France, in the Eastern Pyrenees, Merton was the older son of Owen and Ruth Jenkins Merton, a New Zealand painter and an American dancer. His parents had met in Paris four years before "Tom" was born. After his mother died, when he was six years old, he was reared in England, France, and on Long Island. The death of his father during his teenage years—and of his brother in the Second World War—undoubtedly influenced his eventual choice of a vocation, at least up through his early manhood. After entering Clare College, Cambridge University, in 1933, he moved to the U.S., and at Columbia University made a number of close literary friendships—including Robert Giroux and James Laughlin—that remained important the rest of his life. By 1940, he had already published reviews in the New York *Times* and poems in several periodicals.

In 1941, following a conversion to Roman Catholicism at Columbia, Merton left New York for the Trappist monastery in Kentucky where he was ordained in 1949 as Father M. Louis. His *The Seven Storey Mountain* (1948), a selective autobiography that focused on his conversion, sold 600,000 copies in the original hardcover; admired by Evelyn Waugh and Graham Green, it made Merton internationally famous. After that, he published numerous books of spiritual writings, meditations, poetry, and, in the 1960s, essays on peace and social justice, all of which remain widely read. Over the years, he served as novice master at the monastery and later lived as a hermit. Although he maintained a prodigious correspondence and occasionally visited friends in New York, he spent his remaining years at Gethsemani. In 1968, at 54, he made a fateful trip to Southeast Asia to meet with Buddhist monks and the Dalai Lama, and died as the result of an accident in Thailand. Merton's influence has been acknowledged by a number of the principal figures in Catholic social teaching and action—including Daniel Berrigan, Jim Forest, Ernesto Cardenal— who cite as especially important his letters to them.

Although hardly significant as works of art, Merton's poems are interesting in their foreshadowing of ideas and concerns that inform his later essays. "Original Child Bomb" (1961), with its forty-one verses "for meditation to be scratched on the walls of a cave," is one example. A brief history of events leading to Hiroshima, it describes the fascination, even exhilaration with which people involved in making and deploying the bomb responded to it. "What poor, dumb things we are to cooperate so enthusiastically in our own undoing," Merton seems to say.

In meditation 32, he focuses on the explosion itself:

The fireball was 180,000 feet across. The temperature at the center of the fireball was 100,000,000 degrees. The people who were near the center became nothing. The whole city was blown to bits and the ruins all caught fire instantly everywhere, burning briskly. 70,000 people were killed right away or died within a few hours. Those who did not die at once suffered great pain. Few of them were soldiers.

American airmen, reacting to the event (in meditation 33) "thought of/ the people in the city and they were not/ perfectly happy. Some felt they had done wrong. But in any case they had obeyed orders. 'It was war.'" More startling, for Merton, than the war mentality that produced the bomb was the religious language used by the Japanese, unknowingly, in naming it ("Original Child" bomb) and by others, knowingly, in reporting its effects (meditation 34):

> Over the radio went the code message that the bomb had been successful: "Visible effects greater than Trinity....Proceeding to Papacy." Papacy was the code name for Tinian.

Here and elsewhere, the satiric tone of the verse reflects the irony, sadness, and anger that characterize Merton's later reflections on peace and war.

Much as he loved the church and his religious community—or perhaps *because* he loved them—he ridicules the pretention and scandal associated with its "just war" theories, its blessing of the cannons. An admired and devoted communicant, he wrote at a time when his interpretation of the implications of Catholic social teachings and obligations were not widely held—indeed, when such views "were highly suspect and, to some of our fellow Catholics, probably on the fringes of heresy," as his editor and co-worker Gordon Zahn says.

Rereading Merton's later writings, particularly, one is struck by their power and simplicity, their honesty and subtlety—achieved, his biographers suggest, at considerable cost to himself. A quarter-century after his death, they remain among our most important writings on nonviolence, as he remains a significant witness to humane values.

BY THOMAS MERTON
Gandhi on Nonviolence. Thomas Merton, ed. New York: New Directions, 1965.

The Nonviolent Alternative. Gordon Zahn, ed. New York: Farrar, Straus, and Giroux, 1975, 1980.

Zen and the Birds of Appetite. New York: New Directions, 1968.

ABOUT THOMAS MERTON
Furlong, Monica. *Merton: A Biography.* San Francisco: Harper & Row, 1980.

Mott, Michael. *The Seven Mountains of Thomas Merton.* Boston: Houghton Mifflin, 1984.

War or Peace? The Search for New Answers. Thomas Shannon, ed. Maryknoll, N.Y.: Orbis Books, 1980.

DAVID DELLINGER
1915-

FOR A MAN BORN INTO A REPUBLICAN FAMILY WHO claims that all he knew about as a young man was "sports and girls," David Dellinger has been remarkably unpredictable, even revolutionary. Although his refusal to register for the draft in 1940 is usually cited as the beginning of his activist life as pacifist and socialist, he was already committed, at 25, to justice issues, including efforts to gain political asylum for Jews and antifascists escaping from Hitler's Germany. He had been anti-Nazi in "a naive and inexperienced way," he wrote later, after realizing that the U.S. under Franklin Roosevelt "imposed an arms embargo on democratic Spain," but failed to stop American corporations "shipping oil, scrap iron, and munitions all over the world, including fascist Japan."

The irony of our government's attacking policies of dictatorial governments while supporting them with money and munitions was not lost on the young ministerial student. It's a contradiction that has influenced his vocation as one of the most faithful apostles of nonviolence in U.S. history.

Born in Wakefield, Massachusetts, on August 22, 1915, to an educated, conservative New England family, David Dellinger, like his father—a Boston lawyer—graduated from Yale University. After spending a year at New College, Oxford, he returned to Yale Divinity School. In 1939, he moved to New Jersey as an associate minister and began studies at Union Theological Seminary in nearby New York City.

Already a pacifist, Dellinger was imprisoned in 1940 for a year and a day at Danbury (Conn.) Federal Prison for refusing to register for the newly initiated draft—although he would have qualified for a ministerial deferment at the time. Later he served two years at Lewisberg (Penn.) Penitentiary, when he would not report for induction into the armed forces or for an assignment at a Civilian Public Service Camp. At Lewisberg, his commitment to social justice led to his initiating a 65-day hunger strike protesting racial segregation. Ending up in "the hole" (solitary confinement), he learned "that there are no comforts, no luxury, no honors, nothing that can compare with having a sense of one's own integrity—one's knowledge that in his own life, in his own commitment, he is living up to the best that he knows."

While his contemporaries were fighting a war with the Japanese or the Germans, Dellinger was engaged in a demanding struggle at home. In many ways, his physical and moral condition resembled that of Karl Shapiro's conscientious objector, in a poem of that title written during Shapiro's years as a soldier in the South Pacific:

The gates clanged and they walked you into jail
More tense than felons but relieved to find

The hostile world shut out...
A sense of quiet, of pulling down the blind
Possessed you. Punishment you felt was clean.

Acknowledging the contribution of that "mutinous crew...The opposite of all armies," to which Dellinger belonged, Shapiro concludes the poem with a tribute to war resisters: "Your conscience is/ What we come back to in the armistice."

Working briefly as a farm hand and in a factory after his release from prison in 1945, Dellinger spent most of the next two decades "living and working communally" in Newark and in Glen Gardner, New Jersey. In addition to his wife, Elizabeth Peterson, and their five children, his close associates during this period included a "who's who" of advocates for nonviolent social change in the U.S.: A. J. Muste, Bayard Rustin, Paul Goodman, Staughton Lynd, Barbara Deming, Sidney Lens, Marj Swann, Rita and Marty Corbin. Several of them contributed to the periodicals that Dellinger edited and sometimes set in type: *Direct Action, Alternative,* and *Liberation.*

The latter magazine "signalled a new moment in American radical culture and politics, by giving radical pacifism a revolutionary wing," according to Charles DeBenedetti, a leading historian of peace reform movements. In an effort to address "the decline of independent radicalism and the gradual fading into silence of prophetic and rebellious voices" during the Cold War years, Dellinger published important political commentators and artists including Dorothy Day, Michael Harrington, Lewis Mumford, Kenneth Rexroth, and called attention early on to Martin Luther King's leadership in the Civil Rights movement. While editing *Liberation,* Dellinger also worked closely with the War Resisters League and Committee for Nonviolent Action, organizing activities related to disarmament and civil rights.

In the late 1950s, Dellinger joined Ammon Hennacy and others protesting Civil Defense drills in New York City, who argued that the only real defense against nuclear weapons was to stop making them. As a visible and persistent opponent of war, Dellinger served as co-chair of the New Mobilization Committee to End the War in Vietnam and in numerous other key positions in a long, demanding, and ultimately successful campaign. He also traveled to Southeast Asia three times (and again in 1985) and to Paris twice during the war, in important meetings with North Vietnamese officials, including arrangements for the the release of American pilots.

The attitude of those responsible for our Vietnam policy toward Dellinger is suggested by Congressman (later President) Gerald Ford's contention that demonstrations against the Vietnam war were "planned and organized in Hanoi." In one of many efforts to crush the anti-war movement, the U.S. government indicted Dellinger as a member of the Chicago 8 (with Abbie Hoffman, Bobby Seale, Tom Hayden, and others) for conspiring to disrupt the Democratic National Convention in Chicago in 1968. The long and confusing trial was generally characterized by improprieties on the judge's part that led to most of the charges being dismissed; its consequences included the growth of the anti-war movement and considerable public acclaim for the defendants.

Since the end of the war in Southeast Asia in 1975, Dellinger has continued as an activist. In addition to editing *Seven Days Magazine* and freelance writing, he supports initiatives for women's liberation and interracial justice and peace. An important topic of research for this good-natured grandfather and "one man revolution" is Vietnam, involving years of personal experience and study. Looking back at what he calls "mostly unknown history" prior to 1965 in *Vietnam Revisited*, he discusses U.S. policies "that had catastrophic results for millions of Vietnamese and hundreds of thousands of young Americans and their families, lovers, neighbors and friends." As a piece of investigative reporting, the book tells as much about the U.S. as it does about Vietnam, including the consequences "for the twenty-first century (if we survive that long), if we fail to face up to these realities and change them."

Shortly after Dellinger's release from prison in 1945, in a concise, direct statement prompted by "the crowning infamy" of Hiroshima, Dellinger introduced a theme about American culture that he has returned to in speeches and writings ever since. He called for a campaign not only against militarism and conscription, but also against "an economic and social system that supports them." At the same time, he argued that such a "nonviolent war" must be uncompromising in its commitment to treat each person, "including the worst of our opponents, with all the respect and decency that he merits as a fellow human being." Only then will the effort be worthy of the ideals it seeks to serve.

In keeping with this earlier statement, Dellinger regarded the Vietnam war and U.S. nuclear policy as logical expressions of a "profit-oriented economy and self-righteous foreign policy, both of which have been with us from the beginning." Although critical of a culture where "the health of the state conflicts with the health of the citizenry, and the prerogatives of property prevent the fulfillment of the people," Dellinger also acknowledges America's achievements, its promise, in charting and "imaging" the future.

Referring to Randolph Bourne's epigram, "War is the health of the State," then to William James's search for a "moral equivalent of war," Dellinger insists that remaining aloof from justice struggles will bring no politically effective substitute to war. Equally pointless is "a purist condemnation of those who, seeing no alternative," resort to armed struggle in resisting the institutionalized violence of slum, property, and money—in this country or other countries dominated by rich, imperial powers. The alternative, Dellinger says, is an international movement reflecting the needs and hopes of a diverse people, in campaigns conducted, and through conflicts resolved, without killing.

In a long and faithful commitment to the common good, he maintains a vision both utopian and practical about people's ability to choose for themselves without hurting one another. Respected for his intellectual honesty and integrity even by those who reject his radical politics, he works for a social order in which citizens "can do the things that fulfill them, in such a way that they express their dignity, their self-reliance, and their love for each other."

BY DAVID DELLINGER

More Power Than We Know: The People's Movement Toward Democarcy. New York: Doubleday, 1976.

Revolutionary Nonviolence: Essays. Indianapolis: Bobbs Merrill, 1970.

Vietnam Revisited: From Covert Action to Invasion to Reconstruction. Boston: South End Press, 1986.

ABOUT DAVID DELLINGER

DeBenedetti, Charles, and Charles Chatfield. *An American Ordeal: The Anti-War Movement of the Vietnam Era.* Syracuse: Syracuse University Press, 1990.

The Power of the People: Active Nonviolence in the United States. Philadelphia: New Society Publishers, 1987.

WILLIAM STAFFORD
1914-

THE SCENE: A PUBLIC SERVICE CAMP ON THE EDGE OF A
small Arkansas town during World War II. A townsman has just
grabbed the paper on which George, a conscientious objector, is
writing and has said, "If you don't like the town, you haven't any
right to come around here." Slowly, twenty-four more town citizens gather, as one grabs the book a second C.O. is reading, a copy
of Walt Whitman's *Leaves of Grass*, and the board on which a third
is painting a picture. If the townsmen succeed in provoking a bel-
ligerent reaction from any one of them, they will probably beat up

and maybe even lynch the C.O.'s. The three classic peace churches—Brethren, Quakers, and Mennonites—provided support for C.O.'s during this period of alternative service for draft-age war resisters.

Luckily, however, the violence in the scene involving the townsmen and the "outsiders" dissipates when a policeman from nearby Magnolia, Arkansas, happens by, and the crowd disperses. The next day, the conscientious objectors, including William Stafford who wrote a memoir about the incident, gather in their barracks to address these questions: "When are men dangerous? How could we survive in our little society within a society? What could we do?"

"Pacifism evokes a strange kind of aggression sometimes," Stafford has said, explaining his "jujitsu stance for creating, and teaching, and living." He associates that independent spirit with his four years as a conscientious objector during the Second World War, when the incident described above occurred. In the solitude and fellowship among others doing alternate service, he discovered a way of blending the "two rivers" of his life, one made up of events, places, people—social action—and the other of a mysterious inner life. Rising at 4 A.M. helped him to find that "independent channel of the second river."

As a C.O., in Arkansas and California, Stafford also found "down in our hearts" a fellowship which he wanted to protect and to promote "as something more important than—something prerequisite to—any geographical kinship or national identity." That fellowship contrasted greatly with a society rent by war, with its thousands, indeed millions "of broken fellowships, of alienations," he said in the brief, understated memoir of those years. He tells about the misunderstandings, tensions, and risks experienced by pacifists during a "popular" war. Throughout Stafford's *Down in My Heart* (1947), the narrator "talks" to a total resister, "George," who went to prison, while the narrator himself married and took up his life and career after the war.

William Stafford's poems and essays since then, his readings and teaching, may be regarded as attempts to heal a war-torn social fabric and to celebrate modest "nonviolent" ways of being in the world. A central message throughout resembles that of an earlier American writer, Henry David Thoreau: simplify, simplify, simplify.

Born in 1914, in Hutchinson, Kansas, the eldest of three children, to a mother with a "horror of militarism" and a father "addicted to reading," William Edgar Stafford is the author and editor of over thirty books, including *Traveling Through the Dark* (1962), which received the National Book Award for Poetry—the same year that another World War II conscientious objector, J. F. Powers, received the National Book Award for fiction. Since then, Stafford has been honored many times for his contribution to American literature, serving as poetry consultant to the Library of Congress, reading and lecturing throughout this country, in Europe, and the Middle and Far East. Now retired from Lewis and Clark College, Portland, where he taught for almost four decades, he lives with his wife, Dorothy, and near their children, in Lake Oswego, Oregon.

William Stafford was relatively "late" in coming to public attention. After finishing a degree at the University of Kansas in Lawrence, he returned to the University of Kansas for an M.A. degree (and later the University of Iowa, for a Ph.D.) and became a teacher. Although his work is often included in anthologies of contemporary poetry, it is not as inevitable a choice as work by Theodore Roethke or James Wright, Robert Lowell or Sylvia Plath.

Stafford's work is a kind of linguistic representation of the Midwestern/Southwestern landscape, flat, modest, even "barren" by some standards. The speech has a music about it that must be listened for, since it is not the expected American poetic voice, neither formal like Poe's nor highly ambitious like Whitman's; it's more like the early modernist verse of William Carlos Williams— simple, direct, surprising with its effects. For that reason, the "discoveries" we find there seem ours rather than the writer's, "a voice so calm in its spiritual reserves that it lulls any reader into a dreamy curiosity about his own life and surroundings," as Paul Christensen has said. "He is at once all of us and yet his own vinegary individual, patriotic but wary of government, religious but without orthodoxy, modest and yet quick-witted, wise, at times even a visionary."

Sometimes, listening closely, one "gets" a Stafford poem, sometimes not. I have read whole volumes and "found" only a poem or two. As he said himself, "My poetry...is much like talk, with some enchantment. Thomas Hardy is my most congenial poetry landmark, but actually the voice I most consistently hear in my poetry is my mother's voice."

Stafford's talk is not obviously "poetic," as more ambitious writers' talk tends to be. "Passing Remark" is representative:

In scenery I like flat country.
In life I don't like much to happen.
In personalities I like mild colorless people
And in colors I prefer grey and brown.

He seems to want to catch the reader off guard, particularly the smug reader who thinks that only "high sounding" words and phrases carry deep or profound meaning. Stafford slips up on us, like a man tip-toeing around the corner and saying "Boo!" (but not too loud). The reader jumps slightly or tenses up, perhaps smiles or aches just a bit, when he or she "gets" the full implication of a line or a poem.

The subject matter may seem slight, as in "First Grade" or "1932," which has the immediacy of history. Yet the poems sometimes consist of highly sophisticated, even metaphysical reflections, as in "For People with Problems About How to Believe" or "Meditation":

Animals full of light
walk through the forest
toward someone aiming a gun
loaded with darkness.

That's the world: God
holding still
letting it happen again,
and again and again.

In a quick, remarkable insight, Stafford occasionally tells the reader (and himself) to "listen" and "watch" for the intersection of time and eternity:

> Hat pulled low at work,
> I saw the branding iron
> take the first snowflake.

Stafford has defined poetry, and by indirection his own work, as "a serious joke, a truth that has learned jujitsu," with this caution: "Poetry is the kind of thing you have to see from the corner of your eye...like a very faint star. If you look straight at it you can't see it, but if you look a little to one side it is there." Poetry is accessible to everybody, he insists. "Anyone who breathes is in the rhythm business; anyone who is alive is caught up in the imminences, the doubts mixed with the triumphant certainty, of poetry."

What has such a writer to do, one might ask, with nonviolent social change? The answer is that in his poems, Stafford gives one a sense of how nonviolent resistance to injustice "should" be conducted and, at times, a vision of what a culture committed to the welfare of every person feels like. "My impulse, even in protest," Stafford wrote to James F. Mersmann in 1972, "is toward some kind of redemptive move toward the opposition."

"Meditation," quoted above, describes the quiet, distressing violence of "crass causality," in a manner similar to Thomas Hardy's or Robert Frost's. On a more communal, optimistic note, Stafford's poem "Globescope" recommends positive, global values, echoing Walt Whitman. It's one of a series of "social action" verses, intended, as the author says, "to reach out for you and gain your allegiance":

> Grass is our flag. It whispers, "Asia,
> Asia, Dakota, Dakota, Prairie, Steppe."
> All over the world it leans above rivers—
> Volga, Amazon, Ganges—a grass like wheat
> and its friend the wind, carrying our message
> everywhere, leaf by leaf.

It is a good flag. But sometimes others
hover above and all around us,
relying on some great Beowulf satellite
infallibly orbited, loaded with warheads,
patrolling, lashing a laser and ready
against all enemies.

Then, glancing from their high place,
those warriors feel pity for us quelled
millions, hostages to someone or some
policy poised above us. Warriors can't think
that way for long: it does no good
to tolerate waverers.

But grass is our flag, with its little song
carrying a breath, and a pause, and a breath
again, a voice in the world like a mother
holding her child in its cradle and caring—
the song of life that all things utter
to the world's people.

And many will join. The breath of our lives
is a pledge across years to each other:
whatever happens, we are faithful
in that world story where the rivers flow
and the wind discovers its great following,
and the grass whispers.

This manifesto for social change calls us to a quiet revolution, but
a revolution nevertheless. It's the one that William Stafford has
lived for sixty years, as conscientious objector, war resister, peacemaker, poet or—as Shelley put it—"as unacknowledged legislator
of the world."

BY WILLIAM STAFFORD

A Scripture of Leaves. Elgin, Ill.: Brethren Press, 1989.

Down in My Heart. 2nd ed. Swarthmore, Penn.: Bench Press, 1985 (1947).

Stories That Could Be True: New and Collected Poems. New York: Harper & Row, 1977.

Writing the Australian Crawl. Ann Arbor: University of Michigan Press, 1978.

You Must Revise Your Life. Ann Arbor: University of Michigan Press, 1986.

ABOUT WILLIAM STAFFORD

Christensen, Paul. "William Stafford." *Contemporary Poets.* 5th ed. Tracy Chevalier, ed. Chicago: St. James Press, 1991.

ROSA PARKS
1913-

"LOOK, WOMAN, I TOLD YOU I WANTED THE SEAT. ARE you going to stand up?"

"No."

"If you don't stand up, I'm going to have you arrested," the bus driver said.

"I'm not going to move," Rosa Parks said.

Mrs. Parks had had a busy day at her job as a seamstress in a men's clothing store. Her neck and shoulder ached when she got on the bus. It was late afternoon, cold and dark, Montgomery, Alabama, December 1, 1955.

This episode involving Parks sometimes serves to introduce the story not of her life, but of a man who became very famous just after "she would not be moved." The dialogue repeated here, in fact, opens a biography of Martin Luther King, Jr., by David J. Carrow, which received the Pulitzer Prize in 1987.

"I wasn't planning to be arrested at all," Parks admitted later. "I had a full weekend planned. It was December. Christmastime." As a tailor's assistant, she knew the next few weeks would be hectic, with a lot of sewing to do and alterations to make; also, as secretary of the Montgomery chapter of the National Association for the Advancement of Colored People (NAACP), she "was preparing for the weekend workshop of the Youth Council," which she advised.

After James F. Blake, the bus driver, questioned her, policemen came onto the bus to warn Parks that, according to Alabama state law, she had to give up her seat to a white man. "Why do you treat us this way?" she asked. In refusing to stand, she helped to initiate a revolution that changed the South. Her arrest led the very next day to a boycott of the Montgomery buses by 50,000 black people, 75 percent of whom depended upon the public transit.

The boycott led, in turn, to local clergy forming the Montgomery Improvement Association and electing a young man named Martin Luther King, Jr., as its first chair. The twenty-six-year-old son and grandson of preachers and a doctoral candidate at Boston University's School of Theology, King had recently moved to the state capital of Alabama with his wife and young child. He had accepted a call as pastor of Dexter Avenue Baptist Church, a well-known black congregation in the shadow of the State Capitol Building.

The boycott of the buses following Parks' arrest lasted from December 1955 to December 1956, when the Supreme Court declared the law unconstitutional. At that point, Parks rode on a desegregated bus, again with driver James F. Blake. "He didn't react at all," she said later, "and neither did I."

Born February 4, 1913, in Tuskegee, Alabama, Rosa Louise McCauley is the daughter of James and Leona Edwards McCauley, a carpenter and teacher. When she was two, Rosa, her parents, and a younger brother moved to her grandparents' farm in the same state. She remembers "going to sleep as a girl hearing the Klan ride at night and hearing a lynching and being afraid the house would burn down." At eleven, she enrolled in a private industrial school for girls in Montgomery, which had been founded by white women from the North.

In 1932, Rosa McCauley married Raymond Parks, a barber, who had been working in voter registration campaigns and other civil rights causes for several years. Later she attended what is now Alabama State University, in Montgomery, and worked with the Montgomery Voters League, NAACP Youth Council, and other organizations. In 1943, Parks was elected secretary of the local branch of the NAACP; that year, after she had paid her fare at the front, a bus driver had tried to make her leave the bus and enter again by the back door. It was that same bus driver who confronted her on that historic day in 1955.

Although continually threatened and eventually fired from her job, Rosa Parks remained in Montogomery until 1957, a year after the successful bus boycott, when she and her husband moved to Detroit to live near her mother and brother. Her husband had suffered a breakdown in Alabama, and even though she continued fund-raising efforts for NAACP by appearing at rallies around the country, they endured several years of ill-health and low-paying jobs in Detroit. Since 1965, however, Rosa Parks has enjoyed better times. That year, John Conyers, Jr., a Michigan congressman and leader in civil rights, welfare, and anti-war movements, hired her to work in his office, where she meets visitors and assists him with various efforts on behalf of worker assistance.

More recently, in public appearances and occasional articles (particularly in connection with celebrations honoring the memory of Martin Luther King, Jr.), Parks has been recognized for her essential contribution to a movement involving many talented and dedicated people. Among her several projects for the common good is the Rosa and Raymond Parks Institute for Self-Development, initiated in 1987 (ten years after her husband's death), which focuses on "the average child who may profit most from the lessons of history and from programs designed to foster awareness and involvement." One of its programs is the annual

Reverse Freedom Tour, which takes teenagers on bus tours retracing the Underground Railroad, the route that 19th century slaves took to Canada, and visiting sites of the Civil Rights movement, including the spot where Parks "would not be moved."

Rosa Parks was not the first person arrested for refusing to "move to the back of the bus." A famous Supreme Court ruling against school segregation (Brown v. Board of Education of Topeka) in 1954 had given impetus to desegregation efforts in Montgomery; and before Parks' arrest in 1955, when two young women had been arrested, campaigns had been organized around their trials. For various reasons, NAACP and the Women's Political Council, which had also been active on behalf of desegragation, decided not to pursue the cases in court. With Rosa Parks, they decided the time had come. Jo Ann Robinson, a woman active in the campaign, supported that decision because she regarded Parks as a person who could carry the weight of the case into court, someone who was "quiet, unassuming, and pleasant in manner and appearance; dignified and reserved; of high morals and strong character."

Mrs. Parks's husband felt differently. "The white folks will kill you, Rosa," he told her; others warned her as well. But thinking her appeal of the $14 fine might "mean something to Montgomery and do some good," Parks agreed to go along with the plan. And of course, it did.

The story of Rosa Parks is powerful for a number of reasons, in part because of her quiet courage and patience in accepting the risks associated with her arrest. Equally impressive and essential, however, is the preparation she made for that moment in the years preceding it: the day-to-day, modest assignment and tedious hours as secretary of the NAACP; the educational outreach with the Youth Council; meetings with Myles Horton and Septima P. Clark at the Highlander Folk School, a Tennessee training institute for organizers; even—as she has suggested—her choice of a husband. (She knew of his work before their marriage in defense of the Scottsboro Boys, nine black youths unfairly convicted of raping a white woman in 1931.)

As a person and historical figure, Rosa Parks dramatizes a fact evident in the history of nonviolent social change: the "ordinariness" of those responsible for momentous changes in human events—an "ordinariness" that is also extraordinary. An accident of history—the time, place, and person responsible for a turn of events—is almost never quite an accident, but a coming together of diverse and conscious forces. One person seizes the moment or several people nudge it toward the best possible conclusion. Gandhi did that, in initiating a famous march to the sea, which in turn challenged British authority in India and ended with India's independence; Ammon Hennacy and Dorothy Day did it, in encouraging nonviolent disobedience against civil defense drills, which in turn led to nuclear test ban treaties between the U.S. and the Soviet Union; Martin Luther King, Jr., did it, in recognizing Rosa Parks's contribution and learning as quickly as possible what Glenn Smiley and Bayard Rustin taught about orchestrating a large-scale nonviolent movement to end segregation in the South.

How often we relearn that social change comes not from one action or one person—though that one courageous act or astute person may "spark" a freedom movement, as the song, "Sister Rosa," says. Effective and lasting social change comes, ultimately—as Rosa Parks and the Civil Rights movement demonstrate—from action, cooperation, community that are sustained and carried on by "ordinary people" and "ordinary actions" in "ordinary times."

BY ROSA PARKS
Rosa Parks: Mother to a Movement. New York: Dial Books, 1992.

ABOUT ROSA PARKS
Taylor Branch. *Parting the Waters: America in the King Years 1954-63*. New York: Simon and Schuster, 1988.

Carrow, David J. *Bearing the Cross: Martin Luther King, Jr., and the Southern Christian Leadership Conference.* New York: William Morrow and Co., 1986.

Ragghianti, Marie. "'I Wanted to Be Treated Like a Human Being," *Parade Magazine,* January 19, 1992, 8-9.

"Rosa Parks," *Current Biography Yearbook,* 1989, pp. 431-34.

HELDER CAMARA
1909-

You have a gun
And I am hungry

You have a gun
because
I am hungry

You have a gun
therefore
I am hungry

THE SPEAKER'S TONE OF VOICE, IN M. C. ACRE'S POEM, IS well-known to Dom Helder Camara. Native to one—and formerly archbishop to another—of the poorest, most "feudal" regions of Brazil, he recognizes suffering resonant in the voices of landless peasants. Facts such as the following, involving millions of his people, have shaped his ministry for forty years: $100 income per capita, 70 percent illiterate and with an infant mortality rate of 50 percent. Long before the Second Vatican Council led Latin American bishops at Medellin (1968) and Puebla (1979) to commit themselves to "a preferential option for the poor," Helder Camara had done so.

Faithfulness to the poor, a theme of his poetry and prose, has inspired advocates for social justice throughout the world, and his work has evoked awards and honorary degrees, as well as several nominations for the Nobel Prize. (In 1973, the year the Nobel Prize for Peace went to Henry Kissinger and Le Duc Tho, European workers, students, and others gave an "alternate" People's Peace Prize of $300,000 to Camara.) In organizing base communities and initiating the National Conference of Brazilian Bishops (CNBB) in 1952, he helped to reclaim a voice for the Brazilian church and its people. The Movement for Grassroots Education, another project, "developed over a thousand church-sponsored radio schools that brought poor people together in literacy circles in which they critically examined the region's poverty, malnutrition, and illiteracy," according to Penny Lernoux's *Cry of the People*. Lernoux described the consequences of this movement when a repressive government, under a policy of "national security," terrorized peasants, lay and clerical ministers, who were associated with Christian renewal throughout Latin America.

Basic tools for Camara's educational movement were the Bible and the educational philosophy of his fellow Brazilian, Paulo Freire, in *Pedagogy of the Oppressed*. After a period of reform associated with that movement, Catholics influenced by it resisted the repression that followed a military coup in Brazil in 1964, the year Camara became archbishop of Recife. In that period, his life was threatened many times, his house machine-gunned, his name slandered, as the Brazilian media banned and blacklisted him for nine years. The man who endured this harrassment is the same one whose poem, written about the same time, said:

Hope without risk
is not hope,
which is believing
in risky loving,
trusting others
in the dark,
the blind leap....

Five feet four inches tall, weighing 120 pounds, Helder Pesoa Camara is often characterized as "frail," with an energetic manner and an animated speaking style. Born February 7, 1909, in Fortaleza, on the northeastern coast of Brazil, he was one of thirteen children of a devout Catholic mother and a father who taught that "it is possible to be good without being religious." As a boy of fourteen, Camara entered the seminary nonetheless, was ordained in 1931, and spent the next five years as a priest in his native city. Attracted to the "Green Shirts," a Brazilian fascist party, because of its militant anti-communism, he says that his naivete at that time makes it easier for him to understand others similarly misled.

Transferred to Rio de Janeiro in 1936, Camara gradually came to realize "the fallaciousness of the communism-anticommunism dichotomy." All around him were people ill and underfed, living in shacks and without hope. "They suffer the consequences of an extremism—a massive hysterical anticommunism," dramatizing the fact that "the most threatening clash of our time is not between East and West but rather between the developed and underdeveloped countries," he wrote later. Much of the suffering, represented by a high incidence of tuberculosis in his own region, arises from the rich maintaining their wealth while crushing their fellow citizens, he said. Injustices result, not just from "occasional events," but from structures, he said in 1977 in Washington, D.C., including corporations that cover the world and sometimes "ally themselves to military power and to governments."

Appointed auxiliary bishop of Rio de Janeiro in 1952, Camara founded the National Conference of Brazilian Bishops shortly afterward. Already, he was widely respected by lay and clerical leaders for his work in the slums and his sponsorship of cooperative apartments for poor families. As a participant in the Second

Vatican Council, he announced that he was eager to see the church go boldly "in search of her lost poverty." Even during that Council, in the 1960s, however, the Roman curia censored him when he suggested that the episcopate address social issues more directly. In response to their action, he circulated an open letter to his brothers at the Council urging them to forego privileges and decorative attire that scandalize and distance working-class Catholics from the clergy.

Named archbishop of Olinda and Recife by Paul VI (the same year that the military overthrew a reformist president in Brazil), Camara initiated the Action, Justice, and Peace Association to support a just wage among workers earning less than $350 a year. Addressing students at the Catholic University of Pernambuco, Brazil, the new archbishop spoke of his obligation, his right and duty, to sound such warnings, "to denounce whenever it is necessary, to stimulate, to question, to suggest, to discourage, to encourage," on the basis of the fact "that the fate of people is at stake, and they are our people, flesh of our flesh, blood of our blood."

As conditions worsened under a repressive government, Camara's close associate—and chaplain to the students at the University of Recife—was murdered; terrorists machine-gunned Camara's residence and terrorized other progressives in the city. After the death of Paul VI, the Roman curia moved against Camara once again, criticizing his leadership, including his associates and admirers, who included several liberation theologians and fellow bishops.

Throughout the campaign to discredit him, Camara has insisted that the inspiration for his program for improving the lot of workers and peasants comes not from the writings of Karl Marx, but from papal encyclicals and Catholic social teaching. Or as a well-known poster of him says, "When I give food to the poor, they call me a saint. When I ask why the poor have no food, they call me a communist." During a meeting of fellow clerics in Lima, Peru, he stood once in tears before other Latin American bishops, pleading with conservatives among them to stop playing into the hands of dictators by calling liberation theology "communist inspired." Influenced by "the politics of greed," as Alfred Kazin calls it, of the Reagan/Bush administrations, clerical and government leaders in the U.S. repeated the same charge.

During the Cold War and since, Camara has been critical of the super powers, "supreme examples of capitalism and socialism, [who] remain blind and deaf, enclosed and imprisoned in their egoism...Today 85 percent, tomorrow 90 percent, rot in misery in order to make possible the excessive comfort of 15 percent, tomorrow 10 percent of the world's population. Who cannot fail to understand the need for a structural revolution in the developed world?" he asked in 1967.

Michele Pellegrino, Archbishop of Turin, in his introduction to Camara's *The Church and Colonialism: The Betrayal of the Third World*, described his "frank and fervent word" as a worthy continuation of "the tradition of Basil, Ambrose, Chrysostom," early doctors of the church, and asked that it "arouse an uneasiness which may lead to a new search for the way of justice, love and peace." Although retired—and replaced by a prelate less concerned about the issues that informed his predecessor's public ministry—Dom Helder Camara remains "a presence" in Brazil and wherever the church lives out its "preferential option for the poor." In his visits to the United States (and in an excellent film, *Excuse Me, America*, about Camara, Dorothy Day, and Cesar Chavez, at the 1978 Eucharistic Congress in Philadelphia), he inevitably calls attention to suffering in this country that so frightfully resembles the consequences of injustice in his own.

BY HELDER CAMARA
The Church and Colonialism: The Betrayal of The Third World, tr. William McSweeney. Denville, N.J.: Dimension Books, 1969.

The Desert Is Fertile. Dinah Livingstone, tr. Maryknoll, N.Y.: Orbis Books, 1974.

ABOUT HELDER CAMARA

De Broucker, Jose. *Dom Helder Camara: The Violence of a Peacemaker*, tr. Herma Briffault. Maryknoll, N.Y.: Orbis Books, 1970.

Lindsay, Jane Dubs. "No Longer a Saintly Figurehead." *Sojourners*, VI, 10, (September 1977), 19-23.

Hope, Marjorie, and James Young. *The Struggle for Humanity: Agents of Nonviolent Change in a Violent World*. Maryknoll, N.Y.: Orbis Books, 1977.

Lernoux, Penny. *Cry of the People: United States Involvement in the Rise of Fascism, Torture, and Murder and the Persecution of the Catholic Church in Latin America*. New York: Doubleday, 1980.

_____. *People of God: The Struggle for World Catholicism*. New York: Viking Press, 1989.

Franz Jagerstatter
1907-1943

Consider two things: from where, to where
Then your life will have its true meaning.

"THE REFUSAL," THE TITLE OF THE GERMAN FILM ABOUT
his life, captures the spirit of the drama: an Austrian peasant's
personal, but firm resistance to a despotic government. Although
state and ecclesiastical authorities advised him to do as he was
told, Franz Jagerstatter refused to support an unjust war. He suffered death rather than perform military service in Hitler's army.

Writing in a small composition book, in pencil, shortly before he was beheaded, he asked:

> For what purpose, then, did God endow all men with reason and free will if, in spite of this, we are obliged to render blind obedience; if, as many also say, the individual is not qualified to judge whether this war started by Germany is just or unjust? What purpose is served by the ability to distinguish between good and evil? I would be ready to exhibit unquestioning obedience, but only in circumstances where one would not be hurting others by doing so.

No one would be more surprised than Franz Jagarstatter at his present fame: not only from a well-known biography and several films, but also as a result of war resisters who regularly quote his journal in their applications for conscientious objection or in court, following arrests for civil disobedience against nuclear weapons. Recently, the president of Austria declared Jagerstatter a national hero; and authorities of the Roman Catholic church—in contrast to their wartime counterparts, who recommended that Jagerstatter ignore his conscience—are seriously considering his cause for canonization.

Born May 20, 1907, in St. Radegund, a small Austrian village near Bavaria, Franz Bachmeier was reared by his mother and stepfather. When his father was killed in the First World War, his stepfather, after marrying Franz's mother, adopted him, and later gave over his farm to him. Growing up, Franz Jagerstatter attended school in his home village, and as a young man gained a reputation for being robust, fun-loving, even rowdy.

In 1936, he married a woman from a village nearby; they went to Rome on their honeymoon. Born a Catholic, like everyone else in the village, Jagerstatter experienced a kind of religious conversion around this time, influenced perhaps by his devout wife. Over the next few years, when their three daughters were born, he became increasingly active in the small 15th-century parish church, where he served as sexton.

In 1938, when Hitler's army moved across the German border into Austria, Jagerstatter was apparently the only person in the village to vote against the take-over. His was a singular, personal resistance, without any link to a political party or movement. Although he realized that clergy opposing the *Anschluss* might lose their religious freedom, he was discouraged by their voting for the National Socialists. The choice, he said later, was not much different from the one offered to the crowd on Maundy Thursday between "the innocent Saviour and the criminal Barabbas." Gradually, Jagerstatter gave up arguing politics with his friends over beer—then cider—at the local inn, and responded to their greeting "Heil Hitler!" with "Pfui Hitler!"

Although he took part in some military training, Jagerstatter remained publicly anti-Nazi. When he was finally called to active duty in February 1943, he stuck with his plans, related earlier to his friends, to refuse to put on a uniform, even after they and the local priest told him it was folly to resist. His closest friend remembered saying "Go with God, Franz," the day he left the village, and his response, "You'll see no more of me."

A month later, while he was imprisoned at Linz, Jagerstatter wrote his wife that he had recently taken the difficult step of saying "No!" once again, and thanked her "for all the love and fidelity which you have brought me and the whole family. And for all the sacrifices you must still undergo for my account." At this time, the Bishop of Linz spelled out to Jagerstatter "the moral principles defining the degree of responsibility borne by citizens and private individuals for the acts of the civil authority."

Shortly afterward, Jagerstatter was transferred to a prison in Berlin, where he stood for a military trial on July 6, 1943. Sternly lectured by two high-ranking officials about his obligations to serve the Fatherland, he responded that he was well aware of the penalty, but he could not serve the regime.

Quotations from Jagerstatter's letters at this time are very moving, reflecting his obvious love for the countryside near his farm and his concern for conflicting obligations—as his neighbors regarded them—between his family and his conscience:

Again and again people stress the obligations of conscience as they concern my wife and children. Yet I cannot believe that, just because one has a wife and children, he is free to offend God by lying (not to mention all the other things he would be called up to do). Did not Christ Himself say, "He who loves father, mother, or children more than Me is not deserving of my love?"

Though considered an enemy of the state, Jagerstatter appears to have been treated with consideration in prison, perhaps because of his sincerity, and the attorney appointed to defend him made an extraordinary effort to get him to recant. The lawyer arranged for Jagerstatter's pastor and wife to visit even after the trial, on July 15. About this time, he wrote, "These few words are being set down here as they come from my mind and my heart. And if I must write them with my hands in chains, I find that much better than if my will were in chains."

Several other Jagerstatter statements have great resonance for anyone concerned about the reluctance of private citizens, political and religious leaders to resist the rise of militarism and the nuclear threat since World War II. Almost as a challenge to what has been called "psychic numbing" (people's tolerance of nuclear destruction), Jagerstatter wrote, "One often hears it said these days that 'if it's all right for you to do this or that with an untroubled mind: the responsibility for what happens rests with someone else.' And in this way responsibility is passed on from one man to another. No one wants to accept responsibility for anything."

His last statements reflect as well the depth of his sanity and holiness, with numerous references to the basic truths of religious faith that seem ever radical, ever new: "The true Christian is to be recognized more in his works and deeds than in his speech. The surest mark of all is found in deeds showing love of neighbor....Let us love our enemies, bless those who curse us, pray for those who persecute us. For love will conquer and will endure for all eternity."

Franz Jagerstatter was beheaded on August 9, 1943, and his ashes are buried in the churchyard in his native village. In a letter written only hours before his death, he promises his children, "I will surely beg the dear God, if I am permitted to enter heaven soon, that he may also set aside a little place in heaven for all of you."

In the village of St. Radegund, pilgrims make their way to his gravesite, particularly since the appearance of Gordon Zahn's biography, *In Solitary Witness: The Life and Death of Franz Jagerstatter* (1962). An American sociologist, Zahn is perhaps the most influential figure in the U.S. on Catholic social thought; he happened upon Jagerstatter's story almost by chance during research for an earlier book, *German Catholics and Hitler's War* (1962), a study of Catholic complicity with the Nazi government. Others credited with preserving Jagerstatter's remarkable story are two priests who knew him: his village pastor, who gathered letters, clippings, and notes about him, and a chaplain at the prison where he went to trial, who wrote articles about Jagerstatter following World War II.

Half a century after his death, these questions about the Austrian peasant, posed by Gordon Zahn, are still relevant: "The facts of Franz Jagerstatter's life may be stated briefly, but how does one begin to tell his real story? What was there about this man that, alone among his friends and neighbors, perhaps alone among all his Austrian co-religionists, made it possible for him to come to his fateful decision?" In an era prejudiced toward violence and killing, Jagerstatter's life remains as one of the most remarkable examples and gifts of nonviolent suffering and courage. How many lives might have been saved over 2000 years if Christians had refused to kill?

ABOUT FRANZ JAGERSTATTER

Zahn, Gordon C. "Clarifying the Disputed Witness of Franz Jagerstatter," *New Oxford Review*, September 1991, 14-19.

_____. *German Catholics and Hitler's War*. Foreword by Daniel Berrigan. New York: E. P. Dutton and Co., 1969 (1962).

_____. *In Solitary Witness: The Life and Death of Franz Jagerstatter*. Springfield, Ill.: Templegate, 1991 (1964).

LU XUN
1881-1936

"LIES WRITTEN IN INK CAN NEVER DISGUISE FACTS WRITten in blood," Lu Xun said of political repression in China. He issued this warning in 1926, just after police in Beijing shot into a crowd of student protesters, killing 40 of them. Sixty-three years later, again in Beijing, the government ordered similar killings, and allies of the victims cited Lu Xun's warning about the consequences of such injustice.

In China's century-long struggle to enter modern history, Lu Xun and other artists served as mediators between the ancients and the moderns. Half a century after his death, amid numerous political twists and turns, he remains a major voice in "the search for modern China," as Jonathan Spence calls it. His brief history of Chinese fiction, published in 1925, retains its reputation as a classic; and he is regarded as a founder of modern literature, and the country's most renowned social critic, even by the present regime.

Lu Xun's distinctive contribution to literature arose from his understanding and appreciation of Chinese culture and his critique of what he regarded as its evasions and cruelties. For this reason, among others, he belongs in that special gallery of figures whose life and writings have been central to resistance movements against humiliation and injustice. In a 1933 essay on how he came to write stories, he said that he drew his materials "from among the unfortunate people of a sickly society with the aim of revealing the diseases and pains, and of calling attention to their cure." Like Jonathan Swift and similar satirists, Lu Xun exposed the horrors of one people's oppression by another—in his case, the Chinese by the Japanese; but he reserved his most biting satire for horrors inflicted by his own countrymen and women on one another.

Lu Xun (the pen name of Zhou Shuren) was born to an educated family in Shaoxing, Zhejiang province, southwest of Shanghai, on September 25, 1881. After a traditional education in Confucian schools for the state examinations, he studied at a Westernized naval academy in Nanjing, and at twenty-one followed a pattern of Chinese intellectuals of the period, by going to Japan for professional training. By that time, his reading of 19th-century English writers, the poetry of Lord Byron, the science fiction of Jules Verne, and the essays of Thomas Huxley on evolution and ethics, had deepened his concerns about his country, including its wasteful bureaucracies and its oppression of women. In China, he said, "starving to death is a small matter, but losing one's chastity is a great calamity." And in a series of acts foreshadowing his vocation as a revolutionary writer, Lu Xun cut off his queue—a long pigtail worn by Chinese men during the Qing dynasty and regarded as a symbol of shame by Chinese nationalists—and gave up a study of medicine to devote full-time to literature.

An incident that occurred during his late 20s symbolized to

him "the sickness of the Chinese people" and contributed to his education as a social critic. In a lantern slide of Japanese executing a Chinaman (accused of being a traitor during the Russian and Japanese war of 1905), a large, apathetic crowd of Chinese looked on. The crowd's behavior suggested to him how his countrymen and women had distanced themselves from their own suffering. And in numerous short stories and essays, he ridiculed what he regarded as the moral confusion of the Chinese, including their toleration of injustices at the hands of Western imperialists, Chinese warlords, and political opportunists. Being humiliated by foreigners is not the same as being humiliated by our own people, he said, for

> if a man slaps his own face, he will not feel insulted, whereas if someone else slaps him, he will feel angry. However, when a man is so cretinous that he can slap his own face, he fully deserves to be slapped by any passerby.

Initially, Lu Xun translated European and Russian works of socialist realism in an effort to make modern political ideas accessible to Chinese readers. His early fiction dates from 1918, when he worked as a librarian and a teacher of Chinese literature in several colleges and universities in Beijing. He came to public notice as the author of "The Diary of a Madman," a short story that portrayed China as a culture that devours her own people. "It has only just dawned on me that all these years I have been living in a place where for four thousand years human flesh has been eaten," the narrator says at one point. In a final lament, he addresses the reader directly: Perhaps there are still children who haven't eaten men? Save the children.... He then asks, "How can a man like myself, after four thousand years of man-eating history—even though I knew nothing about it at first—ever hope to face real men?"

By 1926, when he settled in Shanghai, Lu Xun was generally regarded as the finest short-story writer of his age. Over the next decade, until his death in 1936, he wrote personal and polemical essays, as well as humorous, satiric poems in the classical style, but with contemporary themes.

Rivalry among China's leaders, he argued, only increased the country's vulnerability to foreign aggression. Japan already dominated Korea and parts of China; and Britain, France, Germany, and the U.S. held concessions all along the South China Sea, where foreign law superceded Chinese law. "We're destined to perish wretchedly unless we are willing to be slaves 'without a murmur,'" he complained.

Lu Xun's justly famous and influential "The Story of Ah Qu," took a particularly sardonic view of "the Chinese way" and its inability to reform. "Ah Qu" is a selfish and cowardly man who is killed by the authorities as a revolutionary, though he is only a braggart and thief. Although justice of a kind has been done, the melodramatic and ridiculous attitudes of the townspeople keep them from confronting the emptiness and pettiness of their own lives:

Most people were dissatisfied, because a shooting was not such a fine spectacle as a decapitation; and what a ridiculous culprit he had been too, to pass through so many streets without singing a single line from an opera. They had followed him for nothing.

In an ancient and complex culture, Lu Xun's fiction implies, confusion persists among people bound by tradition, defeatism, and self-delusion. Oppression, for whatever reason, however, should not be tolerated. In the face of it, Lu Xun—like Gandhi—argued that risking violence is preferable to doing nothing. Although most similarities between him and "the mahatma" end there, Lu Xun is probably as important to the emergence of modern China, as Gandhi was to the emergence of modern India.

The tone and message of Lu Xun's poems in the colloquial style are bitingly satiric toward those in power, as well as to the people who tolerated them. In "A Nanjing Story," for example, Chaing-kai Shek, Sun Keh—the son of Sun Yat-Sen, the founder of modern China, and other political rivals stand before Sun Yat-Sen's mausoleum on the outskirts of Nanjing, the capital city, in 1931:

Bigwigs swear in before Sun Yat-sen's tomb

—robbers passing themselves off as saints.
They stand for ten minutes in silent tribute,
each racking his brain, planning to undo the other!

Severely critical of the Koumintang government of the 1930s, Lu Xun kept his distance from the Communists on their way to power, and spent his later years hiding, in Shanghai's Japanese concession, to escape arrest and persecution by various authorities.

Although admired by Mao Tse-tung and lauded, in memory, by the Communist government since 1949, Lu Xun undoubtedly arouses suspicion in the authorities still, as he did in the 1930s. He would have been as vehement in his ridicule of those responsible for the killings near Tiananmen Square in 1989 as he was of the repressive Koumintang in the 1930s. Today's young Chinese, forced to read Lu Xun as a hero of "the revolution," now regard him as a hero of their own resistance to corruption and repression, and contemporary writers and activists regard him as an inspiration for resistance to the bureaucrats of a later time.

Lu Xun is rightfully regarded as one of the great literary radicals by anyone interested in social change. He had a keen eye for injustice and a genius for dramatizing the effects of the lies and circumlocutions of corrupt officials. His interest in the links between language and politics in China during the 1930s make one think of George Orwell's preoccupations with a similar theme in England during the 1940s. And Lu Xun's short stories and poems expose the manipulation of language that accompanies political corruption with a surety resembling Orwell's novels and essays.

Although Lu Xun provided no game plan for reform, he persisted in identifying the confusions and cruelties perpetuated by a corrupt bureaucracy and tolerated by an indifferent populace. He belongs to a tradition of modern writers and pamphleteers around the world—from Thomas Paine to Tolstoi, Gandhi, Orwell, and Paul Goodman—who, living among sleepers, shouted, "Wake!"

BY LU XUN

Selected Works. Yang Xianyi and Gladys Yang, eds. 4 vols. Beijing: Foreign Languages Press, 1956.

Modern Chinese Stories and Novellas 1919-1949. Joseph S. M. Lau, C.T. Hsia, and Leo Ou-Fan Lee, eds. New York: Columbia University Press, 1981.

Poems of Lu Hsun. Huang Hsin-chyu, transl. Hong Kong: Joint Publishing Co., 1979.

ABOUT LU XUN

Kristof, Nicolas D. "China's Greatest Dissident Writer: Dead but Still Dangerous," New York *Times Book Review*, August 19, 1990, 15-16.

Wu-chi, Liu. *An Introduction to Chinese Literature.* Bloomington: Indiana University Press, 1966.

Spence, Jonathan D. *The Gate of Heavenly Peace: The Chinese and Their Revolution, 1895-1980.* New York: Penguin, 1980.

_____. *The Search for Modern China.* New York: W. W. Norton, 1990.

EMMA GOLDMAN
1869-1940

AFTER ORGANIZING AGAINST THE DRAFT DURING THE
First World War, Emma Goldman, Alexander Berkman, and 247
others were deported from the United States in 1919. That repressive measure was a project of an ambitious young lawyer named
J. Edgar Hoover, who regarded Goldman and Berkman, her lover,
as "two of the most dangerous anarchists in this country." Their
principal "crime" was in regarding themselves—as Thomas Paine
and William Lloyd Garrison did before them—as "citizens of the
world." In her commitment to the common good, Goldman fol-

lowed the dictates not of the State, but of her conscience. She took seriously the advice of Walt Whitman in *Leaves of Grass*: "Resist much, obey little./ Once unquestioning obedience, once fully enslaved."

In message and tone, Goldman's introduction to her autobiography (1913), "In Appreciation," is representative. Acknowledging her gratitude to those who came into her life for several hours or several years, she wrote, "Their love, as well as their hate, has gone into making my life worthwhile." In demonstrations, speeches, and vigorous, readable essays, she warned against the dangers of highly centralized power, including the violence and oppression resulting from a managerial elite. As she said in the popular pamphlet "What I Believe" (1908), anarchists were the only ones calling a halt "to the growing tendency of militarism, which is fast making of this erstwhile free country an imperialistic and despotic power." With Eugene Victor Debs, the Industrial Workers of the World, and similar militants in the worker's struggle, Goldman helped to make the period before the First World War perhaps the most vibrant era in American political history. During her adventurous life and since her death, her example has helped to make other lives "worthwhile," as various tributes suggest.

In his *One Man Revolution in America* (1970), Ammon Hennacy named her one of the eighteen greatest Americans, and Dorothy Day, who "longed to walk in the shoes of Mother Jones and Emma Goldman," made Goldman's anarchist principles central to the Catholic Worker movement. Theodore Dreiser regarded Goldman's writings as "the richest of any woman's of the century," and John Dewey and Bertrand Russell thought her an important and attractive personality, as did many European anarchists. The playwright S.N. Behrman wrote affectionately about her in his memoir *The Worcester Account*, and Stanley Kunitz, in the poem "Journal to My Daughter," brags of belonging to "a flinty maverick line," that welcomed Goldman, Ingersoll, and other radicals to the family table, also in Worcester. Howard Zinn, the historian, wrote a successful play about her in the 1970s, and feminist critics regard her as a forerunner of the women's movement. In 1970, young members of the Emma Goldman Brigade marched down

Fifth Avenue in New York City chanting: "Emma said it in 1910/ Now we're going to say it again," according to Alix Kates Shulman.

Born June 27, 1869, in Kovno, Lithuania, Emma Goldman was the third child of Taube Bienowitch, and the first of three children by her second husband, Abraham Goldman. Emma Goldman attended a Jewish elementary school where she excelled academically, before moving to St. Petersburg, where the family's poverty forced her to take a full-time job in a factory at thirteen. Two years later, partly because of her father's threat to marry her off, she fled with her sister to America.

At her first job, in Rochester, New York, Goldman sewed overcoats for ten hours a day at $2.50 a week. In the U.S., as in Russia (where she had seen peasants beaten), she was appalled by the horrible conditions of workers. In 1886, she was deeply affected by the unjust conviction and eventual hanging of four Chicago anarchists in the famous Haymarket Square trial, writing later:

> I had a distinct sensation that something new and wonderful had been born in my soul. A great ideal, a burning faith, a determination to dedicate myself to the memory of my martyred comrades, to make their cause my own.

After a brief marriage to another Russian immigrant and still only twenty years old, she moved to New York City and became the protegee of Johann Most, the anarchist editor of *Freiheit*. Working later as a seamstress, Goldman became a leading organizer for a cloak-maker's strike in 1889. Like many anarchists of the time, she thought that the masses could be aroused to revolt against their masters by some dramatic, polarizing event. In 1892, when Pinkerton guards shot into striking steelworkers at the Carnegie plant, in Homestead, Pennsylvania, Alexander Berkman resolved to assassinate the chairman of the company, Henry Clay Frick. When the attempt failed and Berkman went to prison for fourteen years, Goldman defended him. She became a major spokesperson for anarchism and spent a year in prison for "inciting a riot" that never occurred; in actuality, in an argument resembling that of medieval theologians, she had merely justified the stealing of bread by starving people.

Following a period of repression at the turn of the century (after an anarchist killed President McKinley), Goldman returned to public life again in 1906, the year she launched *Mother Earth*, a monthly supporting feminism, free speech, and similar issues. She published essays on Ibsen, Strindberg, and Shaw, whose plays she regarded as powerful dramatizations of the plight of women, as well as anarchist classics by Kropotkin and Bakunin, writings by Oscar Wilde, and her own essays on anarchism and literature.

While giving herself tirelessly to various campaigns for workers' rights and women's rights, she was also a success on the lecture circuit, speaking 120 times in thirty-seven states during 1910, for example. "Combative by nature," Alix Kates Shulman says, Goldman "talked up free love to puritans, atheism to churchmen, revolution to reformers; she denounced the ballot to suffragists, patriotism to soldiers and patriots." In 1915, she spent fifteen days in jail for giving a public lecture on methods of birth control in support of Margaret Sanger.

When America entered the war against Germany in 1917, Goldman and Berkman—now out of prison—formed the No-Conscription League, which led to their arrest for conspiring to obstruct the draft. The league maintained that "the militarization of America is an evil that far outweighs, in its anti-social and anti-libertarian effects, any good that may come from America's participation in the war." In a characteristically witty and courageous speech to the judges, Goldman described the methods of the arresting officer and "his host of heroic warriors" as being "sensational enough to satisfy the famous circus men, Barnum & Bailey....

A dozen or more heroes dashing up two flights of stairs prepared to stake their lives for their country, only to discover the two dangerous disturbers and trouble-makers, Alexander Berkman and Emma Goldman, in their separate offices, quietly at work at their desks, wielding not a sword, nor a gun or a bomb, but merely their pens! Verily, it required courage to catch such big fish.

(The arresting officers' behavior resembled that of the F.B.I. harassing and arresting draft resisters during the Vietnam war; on Block Island in 1970, for example, Daniel Berrigan was arrested by F.B.I. agents disguised as birdwatchers.)

During the Red Scare of 1919, J. Edgar Hoover, later head of the F.B.I., directed hearings for Goldman's deportation, after revoking her citizenship. Under the 1918 Alien Exclusion Act, he shipped Goldman, Berkman, and 247 other radicals on the *Buford*, an old army transport, to the "new" Soviet Union.

Initially enthusiastic about the Bolshevik Revolution of 1917, Goldman became one of its fiercest critics when she realized that in the U.S.S.R., as in many other countries, anarchists were treated as enemies of the State. Moving to France in the early 1930s, then England, and during the Spanish Civil War to Spain, she directed the anarchist press there. Rising to speak in a crowded hall, amid anarchist cheers, fascist boos, and communist cat-calls, she countered them by announcing "that she had had fifty years of dealing with mobs and no one could shout her down. And by God she was right," says Ethel Mannin, an English novelist, who adds that the crowd sat "enchanted under the attack, and when she had finished applauded wildly."

Traveling to Canada to raise money for Spanish anarchists in 1939, Goldman suffered a stroke and died some months later in Toronto, May 14, 1940. Karl Shapiro, in "Death of Emma Goldman," has pictured her in final moments, surrounded by officials who had hounded her during her adventuresome life:

> Triumphant at the final breath
> Their senile God, their cops,
> All the authorities and friends pro tem
> Passing her pillow, keeping her concerned.

In actuality, she never bowed before authorities and adversaries who denounced, exiled, and imprisoned her; as a great advocate for social justice, loyal to her values and her radical friends, she seldom faltered.

Only in death was Goldman finally allowed to re-enter the United States to be buried in Chicago's Waldheim Cemetery, near the graves of her beloved Haymarket martyrs. Once asked for details about her life, Goldman suggested that the person consult "any police department in America or Europe."

BY EMMA GOLDMAN
Red Emma Speaks: Selected Writings and Speeches of Emma Goldman. Alix Kates Shulman, ed. New York: Vintage Books, 1972.

Living My Life. 2 vols. New York: Dover Publications, (1931) 1970.

ABOUT EMMA GOLDMAN
Drinnon, Richard. *Rebel in Paradise: A Biography of Emma Goldman.* Chicago: University of Chicago Press, 1961.

Falk, Candace S. *Love, Anarchy, and Emma Goldman: A Biography,* Rev. ed. New Brunswick, N.J.: Rutgers University Press, 1990.

JANE ADDAMS
1860-1935

IN 1917, THEODORE ROOSEVELT CALLED HER THE "MOST dangerous woman in America." Five years before, she had seconded his nomination for president as a candidate of the Progressive Party, and he had welcomed her support in his (unsuccessful) campaign. Five years before that, Roosevelt had helped to initiate one of the first inter-governmental peace conferences, a project that she carried further in co-founding the Women's International League for Peace and Freedom.

Theodore Roosevelt, like other conventional Americans, had praised, even admired Jane Addams for co-founding Chicago's Hull House in 1889; but he was shocked when she committed herself to something as "radical" as resisting the war effort in 1915. Such were the shifting, changing responses to one of the great leaders in the American tradition of nonviolence: a person who learned as she went along, taking whatever action seemed appropriate, no matter what the public response.

Although she enjoyed the praise that accompanied her work among poor immigrants, Addams repeatedly risked censure—and the loss of public favor—in addressing the causes of poverty and working for peace during a "popular" war. Her defense of political radicals, especially when the Justice Department imprisoned or exiled them to Europe during the Red Scare of 1919, is particularly noteworthy. "Providing a voice of reason in the midst of hysteria," as Michael A. Lutzger has said, she defended the loyalty of aliens in Chicago and the liberties they had lost:

> The cure for the spirit of unrest in this country is conciliation and education—not hysteria. Free speech is the greatest safety valve of our United States. Let us give these people a chance to explain their beliefs and desires. Let us end this suppression and spirit of intolerance which is making America another autocracy.

Born September 6, 1860, in Cedarville, Illinois, Jane Addams was the eighth of nine children of Sarah Weber and John Huy Addams. Her mother died when Addams was three years old. Her father, a successful miller and eight-term state senator, encouraged Addams to attend Rockford Female Seminary (now Rockville College) near Chicago, where she excelled as a student and won the admiration of her contemporaries. Among various Victorian writers whom she admired, John Ruskin, art historian and social critic, occupied a special place. Following several bouts of ill health in the 1880s, she left Woman's Medical College in Philadelphia after one semester and traveled extensively in Europe on two occasions.

On the second tour, accompanied by Ellen Gates Starr—later a co-founder of Hull House—Addams was deeply impressed by Toynbee Hall, a settlement house in London's East End where university students influenced by Ruskin taught workers and learned from them as well. Although she had long thought about fulfilling an early Christian commitment to the welfare of the poor, she associated her vocation as a social reformer with extensive reading on that subject after her return from England.

Subsequently, Addams and Starr convinced a number of educated women to support their determination to live among the poor in Chicago, where three-fourths of the residents were foreign born. After moving into an old mansion in the heavily populated and predominantly Italian West Side in September 1889, Addams, Starr, and their co-workers provided or arranged for child care, educational programs, and medical assistance for neighborhood immigrants. During the early weeks, they found themselves caring for "a forlorn little baby who, because he was born with a cleft palate, was most unwelcome even to his mother" and later died of neglect, and for "a little Italian bride of fifteen" who sought shelter with them in order to escape her husband's nightly beatings.

> Two of us officiated quite alone at the birth of an illegitimate child because the doctor was late in arriving, and none of the honest Irish matrons would "touch the likes of her"; we ministered at the deathbed of a young man who, during a long illness of tuberculosis, had received so many bottles of whisky through the mistaken kindness of his friends that the cumulative effect produced wild periods of exultation, in one of which he died.

The community of educated women and college students gathered around Hull House provided programs in the arts as well as the elemental necessities for those in need. Faculty from the new University of Chicago (Robert Morss Levett); editors and artists who initiated a "Chicago Renaissance" (Margaret Anderson); socialists and anarchists (Sidney and Beatrice Webb and Peter Kropotkin); workers and scientists "from the river wards of the city" and "from the far corners of five continents": all contributed to the noble experiment and the spirit of community emerging from it. Within four years of the founding of Hull House, Addams and other notable women were assisting and entertaining 2000 people a week in a variety of functions and activities, including theater performances and musical concerts.

In the wider community, Hull House exerted considerable influence on movements for child labor laws, unions, and workers' benefits. In 1909 Addams was elected the first woman president of what would become the National Conference of Social Work; in 1910, she was the first woman to receive an honorary degree from Yale University and published her most widely read book, *Twenty Years at Hull House*, an important autobiography. Traveling extensively in this country and abroad over the next half-century, Addams nonetheless made Hull House her home for the remainder of her life.

Spurred by the enthusiasm of the progressive era, the women's movement, and powerful ideas associated with Early Modernism, Addams had become increasingly interested in international issues. A visit in 1896 with Leo Tolstoy, Russian novelist and Christian anarchist, made a deep impression on her. Although his eating peasant porridge and black bread—while his guests dined in style—made her uncomfortable, she took to heart his teachings about justice and community as the bases of world peace. During the Spanish American War two years later, Addams—like William James, Mark Twain, and Andrew Carnegie—joined the Anti-Imperialist League and began to note the links between violence among Chicago's immigrant poor and violence implicit in America at war.

Haltingly, and in a manner that disconcerted admirers of Hull House, Addams became increasingly involved in efforts to build nongovernmental organizations committed to world peace; inevitably, as a result of these efforts, she became embroiled in controversy. To an impressive social vision linking religious, moral, and aesthetic concerns, Addams added another concern: the disastrous effects of war on social reform.

With the outbreak of the war in August 1914, she worked hard at home and abroad to keep the U.S. neutral so that it might serve as a mediator between the two warring groups. In 1915, as head of the Woman's Peace Party, she traveled the Western front and met with various leaders in an attempt to stop what Ernest Hemingway called "the senseless slaughter."

Over the next two years, Addams watched Woodrow Wilson's gradual drift toward war and the country's increasing belligerence inevitably following it. Wilson and his advisers thought active involvement would strengthen his hand in settling the peace—a belief, as Addams maintained, which turned out to be naive. In the midst of increasing criticism from the Daughters of the American Revolution, American Legion, and similar self-appointed patriots, Addams persisted—as did Eugene Victor Debs, Emma Goldman, Bertrand Russell, Randolph Bourne, and others—in pointing to the disastrous effects of an uncritical endorsement of war policies.

Before the armistice in 1918, Addams was already working to distribute food and to provide relief in war-torn countries. The International Congress of Women, which had met in the Hague during and in Zurich just after the war, included many women who survived the war only to face additional hardships. Warning that the Versailles peace settlement sowed the seeds of another war, the women formed a permanent organization, the Women's International League for Peace and Freedom (WILPF), with Addams as president. In spite of criticism, she continued to work with other groups committed to nonviolence and the protection of human rights, including the American Friends Service Committee (AFSC), American Civil Liberties (ACLU), and National Association for the Advancement of Colored People (NAACP). It was to WILPF, however, that she gave the money accompanying her Nobel Prize for Peace in 1931.

By that time, some of the criticism that had dogged Addams since she announced herself a pacifist in 1915 was muted or forgotten. Never entirely comfortable with her total commitment to nonviolence, she worked persistently, patiently, modestly, nonetheless, to understand its implications for social change. In 1922, describing the isolation she felt among friends supporting the war, she indicated why she remained faithful to that lonely, often misunderstood, nonviolent ethic: "in order to make the position of the pacifist clear it was perhaps necessary that at least a small number of us should be forced into an unequivocal position." In doing so, Addams offered a number of models for "making peace" in a concrete way.

BY JANE ADDAMS

Peace and Bread in Time of War. New York: Garland Publishing Co, (1922) 1972.

Twenty Years at Hull House. New York: Signet Classics, 1960 (1910).

ABOUT JANE ADDAMS

Bussey, Gertrude, and Margaret Times. *Women's International League for Peace and Freedom 1915-1965: A Record of Fifty Years' Work*. London: George Allen & Unwin, 1965.

Davis, Allen. *American Heroine: The Life and Legend of Jane Addams*. New York: Oxford University Press, 1973.

Peace Heroes in Twentieth-Century America. Charles DeBenedetti, ed. Bloomington: Indiana University Press, 1986.

HENRY DAVID THOREAU
1817-1862

"IN THE MOUNTAINS WHERE HENRY DAVID THOREAU preached civil disobedience," the news story began, "some stiff-necked tax resisters are locked in a battle of will with U.S. authorities over an isolated house." In protest against U.S. military interventions around the world, Randy Kehler and Betsy Corner waged "a battle" by refusing to pay federal income taxes on their home. Going Thoreau one better, they gave the tax money to victims of war, homelessness, and injustice.

Subsequently, supporters in the Western Massachusetts village of Colrain risked arrest by occupying the 91-year-old house after Kehler was carried away to jail; in doing so, they joined an estimated 10,000 people throughout the U.S. who resist federal taxes that pay for war and nuclear armaments. Some knowingly, others unknowingly, perhaps, followed the "good ole American" precedent set by Thoreau and others 150 years before.

In 1846, Thoreau was provoked to active resistance by U.S. intervention in Mexico, in this country's first major imperialist war; Kehler and Corner were provoked by U.S. interventions in El Salvador, Panama, Iraq—those successive, relentless imperial sorties during the 1980s, and they were provoked earlier by Korea, Vietnam, Grenada, Nicaragua. Kehler, forty-seven years old at the time of his arrest in December 1991, had spent 22 months in federal prison for draft resistance during the decade-long war in Southeast Asia.

Although Henry David Thoreau regarded himself as a mystic and natural philosopher, he has probably pushed more people into action than have most so-called revolutionaries. Born in 1817 in Concord, Massachusetts, Thoreau ventured from his native city only occasionally, but—like his contemporary Emily Dickinson of Amherst—learned more from his relatively circumscribed life than most people learn by traveling the world. His approach to mining nature's secrets during two year's residence at Walden Pond, then along the Concord and Merrimack Rivers, to Maine and Cape Cod remains as valid today as it was in the mid-19th century. "I went to the woods because I wished to live deliberately," he wrote in *Walden*, "to front only the essential facts of life...

I wanted to live deep and to suck out all the marrow of life...to drive life into a corner, and reduce it to its lowest terms, and, if it proved to be mean, why then to get the whole and genuine meanness of it, and publish its meanness to the world; or if it were sublime, to know it by experience, and be able to give a true account of it in my next excursion.

Prior to his two years at Walden Pond in the 1840s, Thoreau had grown up in Concord, graduated from nearby Harvard Col-

lege, then returned to live with his family and to teach school in
Concord, where he also became a close associate of Emerson and
other members of the Transcendental Club and wrote for *The Dial*
magazine. After the sojourn at Walden Pond, he stayed in Concord, writing and making occasional trips to Maine, Cape Cod,
and New York (where he met Walt Whitman), and—in the early
1860s—to the Great Lakes and along the Mississippi River. His
death in 1862, at 45, was caused by tuberculosis.

One can hardly overemphasize the timeliness of Thoreau's
writings at present, as well as in the 19th century. For citizens, he
provides a vigorous, authoritative, and inspiring rationale for resisting a repressive, war-making State. And his work often led
persons very different from Thoreau in temperament and background "to construct peace." Over the past hundred years, that
influence has been acknowledged by nonviolent activists and theorists from Tolstoy and Gandhi to Martin Luther King, Jr., and
Philip Berrigan, by Danes resisting Nazism in the 1940s, and Chinese students waging a pro-democracy movement in 1989.
Reflecting on his night in jail, initially in a lecture, then in the
published essay, "Civil Disobedience," Thoreau advocates an
adamant stand against paying taxes that "enable the State to
commit violence and shed innocent blood." Thoreau seems
particularly angry at his fellow abolitionists, probably including
Emerson, for their failure to take a more militant stand against
slavery. Emerson's uneasiness with Thoreau is evident in several
journal entries at the time, as well as in their (probably
apocryphal) exchange at the Concord jail: Emerson: "Henry, what
are you doing *in there?*" Thoreau: "Waldo, what are *you* doing out
there?"

Thoreau spoke not as a lawyer or politician, but as a moralist,
because, as he said in *Walden*, "Our whole life is startlingly moral.
There is never an instant's truce between virtue and vice.
Goodness is the only instrument that never fails." He understood
that those most responsible for an evil—at that time,
slavery—succeed not because of their commitment, but because
others who recognize the evil do nothing to stop it. "Practically
speaking, the opponents of a reform in Massachusetts are not a
hundred thousand politicians at the South," he said, "but a

hundred thousand merchants and farmers here, who are more interested in commerce and agriculture than they are in humanity."

In "Civil Disobedience," Thoreau also challenged passive citizens who think they can have a better society merely by wishing for it. "Even voting for the right is doing nothing for it," he argued. "It is only expressing to men feebly your desire that it should prevail." Writing in his journal soon after his night in jail Thoreau said of tepid citizens, "Better are the physically dead for they more lively rot."

Rereading "Civil Disobedience," one imagines what he might say about the politics of greed and the accompanying collapse of this country's infrastructure in the latter decades of the 20th century. The fact that contemporary writers of Thoreau's stature seldom attend to today's civil disobedients as closely as he did to those of his own time tells also of America's decline.

One can hardly take up "Civil Disobedience" without the blood stirring, without being drawn into the central issues of Thoreau's era and our own—issues that touch on the nature not only of government, community, individual rights, but also of language, discourse, writing, argument, rhetoric. It is such a splendid document—vigorous, concrete, passionate, witty, philosophical, even as it provokes more questions about governance, perhaps, than it answers.

Historically, Thoreau's statement belongs to a tradition that dates from at least the 17th century and touches on arguments and cases that involved the Quakers particularly, over three centuries, in England and America. He also profited from and built upon many statements similar to his own in the years associated with the abolitionist struggle and protests against the Mexican War, by Emerson, Bronson Alcott, and the transcendentalists, as well as William Lloyd Garrison and Adin Ballou. It is no accident that, in resisting imperial wars and policies since the Second World War, activists inevitably re-work some of the ground plowed by Thoreau 150 years before.

For centuries, men and women committed to nonviolence have tried to figure out ways not only to resist a system that upheld slavery and oppression, but also to prevent this country from imitating European imperialists in conducting their affairs. Although not the first such effort (David R. Weber, in *Civil Disobedience in America: A Documentary History*, includes several essays written prior to Thoreau's), "Civil Disobedience" brought together the arguments proposed by others in an eloquent and economical way; it remains, along with the Declaration of Independence and Martin Luther King, Jr.'s "Letter from Birmingham Jail," the most influential document in the tradition. Even if Thoreau was not a pacifist, his stance before the State was more revolutionary than those of most recent nonviolent activists, and his argument and statement are central to anyone committed to bringing about social change.

Just how far Thoreau would go to resist the government is dramatized by his "A Plea for Captain John Brown," written a decade after "Civil Disobedience." Reflecting the intellectual and moral vigor of the 1850s, when Emerson, Hawthorne, Melville, and Whitman published other American masterpieces, the essay took the position shared by William Lloyd Garrison, Frederick Douglass, and others who came to regard the Civil War as a holy war against slavery.

In his visits to Worcester, a hot-bed of abolitionism twenty miles southwest of Concord, for example, Thoreau spoke to a sympathetic audience. Thoreau's admirers there included Thomas Wentworth Higginson, Elihu Burritt, Abigail Kelley and Stephen Symonds Foster, and other militants. Some Worcesterites, as with Bostonians and Concordians, probably found Thoreau's "A Plea for Captain John Brown," about the militant abolitionist's raid at Harper's Ferry, too radical for their taste. But characteristically, Thoreau felt compelled "to correct the tone and statements" of editors and politicians regarding Brown's character and actions. In his address, Thoreau told his audience at Mechanics Hall, Worcester, "It costs us nothing to be just."

Hardly a disciple of nonviolence, Thoreau, nonetheless, belongs to an American tradition of justice-seekers that includes John Woolman, Jane Addams, Dorothy Day, Ammon Hennacy, and David Dellinger. And since about 1960, civil disobedients—draft resisters, the Catonsville Nine, members of Clamshell Alliance and Plowshares—have regarded Thoreau as their inspiration and guide. By their commitment to civil disobedience, in resisting injustice and war, they keep Thoreau's memory alive.

Modern scholars, including Walter Harding and Richard Lebeaux, have done their part as well, in enabling us to see the life and thought of the great moralist in context. It remains for the rest of us to see that Thoreau's words and example inform our efforts to alter the priorities of our society and government to reflect his moral and ethical concerns. We do so by resisting unjust laws and practices, as he did, and by "building a new society in the shell of the old," as the Wobblies and Peter Maurin, co-founder of the Catholic Worker movement, recommended. Individual resisters who live Thoreau's principles make a difference, if only "as a majority of one," as he put it.

BY HENRY DAVID THOREAU
Walden and Other Writings. William Howarth, ed. New York: Modern Library, 1981.

Henry D. Thoreau Reform Papers. Wendell Glick, ed. Princeton, N.J.: Princeton University Press, 1973.

ABOUT HENRY DAVID THOREAU
Harding, Walter Roy. *A Thoreau Handbook*. New York: New York University Press, 1959.

Lebeaux, Richard. *Thoreau's Seasons*. Amherst: University of Massachusetts Press, 1984.

Civil Disobedience in America: A Documentary History. David R. Weber, ed. Ithaca: Cornell University Press, 1978.

Civil Disobedience in Focus. Hugo Adam Bedau, ed. New York: Routledge, 1991.

Civil Disobedience: Theory and Practice. Hugo Adam Bedeau, ed. New York: Pegasus, 1969.

ELIHU BURRITT
1810-1879

HOW MANY LIVES WERE SAVED BY JOHN WOOLMAN (1720-72), the abolitionist? How many by Elihu Burritt, "the learned blacksmith" and subject of the present portrait, and other peace activists? Yet students familiar with little-known Civil War officers may never have heard of Woolman and Burritt, while military commanders who sent hundreds to their deaths, in campaigns that neither settled disputes nor furthered just causes, have cities, mountains, and thoroughfares named for them. No wonder that young people sometimes complain, "We learn all about making war, and nothing about making peace."

Famous—or infamous—for its military might and nuclear weapons, the U.S. is also home to important apostles of nonviolence, as well as the first International Peace Society, founded in 1854. Elihu Burritt, one of history's most remarkable advocates of nonviolent social change, was a co-founder of that society; he worked for global peace by encouraging negotiations among countries in conflict and establishing a Congress of Nations to prevent civil and international wars. Although internationally famous in his own lifetime, he remains almost unknown, even in the area of New England where he lived and worked for seventy years.

Born December 8, 1810, in New Britain, Connecticut, he was one of ten children of Elizabeth Hinsdale and the senior Elihu Burritt, a veteran of the Revolutionary War known for his honesty and generosity. "A poor boy," his biographer, Merle Curti, says of the younger Burritt, he shared a life of hardship with his parents, who cultivated "a few rocky, barren acres of soil" in Southern Connecticut. After the death of his father, Burritt apprenticed himself to a village blacksmith, and in the midst of his labors read 18th and 19th century English poetry.

Delighting in the study of languages, according to his own account Burritt "made himself more or less acquainted with all the languages of Europe and several of Asia, including Hebrew, Syriac, Chaldaic, Samaritan, and Ethiopic" by the time he was thirty. Penniless, he had moved to Worcester, Massachusetts, several years before, where he borrowed grammars and lexicons from the American Antiquarian Society, established by the editor and bookseller Isaiah Thomas in 1812. Burritt's journal entry for October 7, 1841, suggests his daily schedule: "Read Ethiopic 1 hour; wrote 1 hour upon a subject which I intend to make a lecture, viz., 'Is Roman patriotism or Christian philanthropy most congenial to the Republican principle?' Got trusted for 30 pounds of cast iron to make my garden hoes of. Went to the library and read 2 1/2 hours. Forged from 1 to 5 P.M. Antislavery Convention in the evening; listened to the most thrilling and powerful speeches."

When Burritt's achievement in languages became known to Edward Everett, Governor of Massachusetts, and Henry Wadsworth

Longfellow, poet and professor of modern languages at Harvard University, Burritt was offered opportunities for formal study, but declined. His vocation, as he described it to Longfellow, was "to stand in the ranks of the workingmen of New England, and beckon them onward and upward...to the full stature of intellectual men."

Through his lectures and writings, Burritt encouraged other young workingmen to study and to develop their talent for scholarship, as he had done. And during his middle and later years, from 1840 until his death in 1879, he devoted himself, as writer, editor, and activist, to campaigns for abolishing slavery and improving workers' conditions, and gathered tens of thousands of signatures for a document in which Europeans and Americans promised never to take up arms against their brothers and sisters again.

From 1844 to 1851, Burritt published *The Christian Citizen*, a newspaper devoted to temperance, abolitionism, and nonviolence. During that period, he addressed International Peace Congresses on three occasions, at Brussels (1848), Paris (1849), and Frankfurt (1850). His speeches called for an international code of justice that might "give the world an ocean penny postage," helping to make the world "home" for everyone and "all nations neighbors." Although his sentiments sound naive at times, and were somewhat circumscribed by his optimistic view of Western thought, they contributed to his later, more sophisticated explorations of nonviolent theory and practice.

From 1865-69, he published the periodical *The Bond of Universal Brotherhood* in the U.S. and in England, where he served as a consular agent at Birmingham during the same period. Burritt's efforts in that post suggest his persistent dedication to the welfare of the poor. He helped to protect prospective immigrants to the U.S., for example, from unscrupulous promoters who took advantage of their clients by misrepresenting working conditions in America.

As editor of the *Advocate of Peace and Universal Brotherhood* for the American Peace Society, Burritt popularized the ideas of William Ladd (1778-1841), founder of the American Peace Society, which helped to shape the League of Nations and the World

Court. More significantly, Burritt emphasized the importance of "people's diplomacy" and is credited with helping to avoid a war with Great Britain over the Oregon Country. Burritt's effort anticipates recent experiments in "citizen diplomacy," in addressing issues related to world hunger, nuclear war, and destruction of the environment. Groups such as Witness for Peace, Bread for the World, Physicians for Social Responsibility, Soviet and Nicaraguan Sister-City Projects, and similar nongovernmental agencies indicate the wisdom of Burritt's approach.

Almost half a century before Mohandas Gandhi and the Industrial Workers of the World (Wobblies) recommended large-scale disobedience against injustice, Elihu Burritt advocated a workingman's strike against war. In a peace pledge of 1867, signed by tens of thousands of Americans and Western Europeans, he wrote, "We hope the day will come when the working-men of Christendom will form one vast Trades Union, and make a universal and simultaneous *strike* against the whole war system."

As did later nonviolent activists (U.S. civil rights workers in the 1950s and 1960s; the June 4, 1989, pro-democracy supporters in China; or those who resisted the 1991 coup in the Soviet Union), Burritt understood the power of nonviolence, "which any community or country might employ successfully in repelling and disarming despotism, whatever amount of bayonet power it might have at its command," he wrote in "Passive Resistance" (1854). His numerous periodicals and thirty books, in the words of Merle Curti, his principal biographer, describe his "manifold efforts to counteract the martial spirit." As with Randolph Bourne, who argued against the U.S. entering World War I so that it might act as an arbitrating power between the warring parties, Burritt wanted the U.S. to act as mediator in the Crimean war. Similarly, Burritt's condemnation of British and French wars in Asia anticipate Gandhi's later speeches on behalf of Indian independence.

In one of his last letters, about "the machinery of war having a central show" in the Philadelphia Centennial Exposition, Burritt indicated a keen, skeptical sense of his country's future. That letter is, in fact, somewhat prophetic of what the U.S. became a century later, as a major supplier of armaments to the world:

For there were never so many furnaces, forges and arsenals at work, turning out the latest improvements in the machinery of war; as at the present moment, and no mind and hand more busy and ingenious in the invention and manufacture of such weapons than the American.

In later years, as his energy waned, Burritt returned to language study, received an honorary degree from Yale University, translated Longfellow's poetry into Sanscrit, and continued writing. *A Voice from the Back Pew* (1870) traced the history of his religious opinions. He died in New Britain, Connecticut, where he was born; there, on the campus of Central Connecticut State University, a library is named for him.

In efforts to resolve conflict, to bring about social change without killing, and to translate peace principles into action, Burritt occupies a special place in U.S. history. For this reason, among others, the historian Staughton Lynd regarded Burritt's life and writings as the most significant contribution to the American tradition of nonviolence between the Revolution and the Civil War.

BY ELIHU BURRITT

The Learned Blacksmith: The Letters and Journals of Elihu Burritt. Merle Eugene Curti, ed; and *A Congress of Nations.* New York: Garland Publishing, 1971.

Thoughts and Things at Home and Abroad. Boston: Phillips, Sampson, and Co., 1854.

Elihu Burritt: A Memorial Volume...With Selections From the Writings and Lectures. Charles Northend, ed. 1979.

ABOUT ELIHU BURRITT

Brock, Peter. *Pacifism in the United States: From the Colonial Period to the First World War.* Princeton, N.J.: Princeton University Press, 1968.

Nonviolence in America: A Documentary History. Staughton Lynd, ed. Indianapolis: Bobbs Merrill, 1966.

Tolis, Peter. *Elihu Burritt: Crusader for Brotherhood.* Archon Books, 1968.

ADIN BALLOU

1803-1890

ALTHOUGH HENRY DAVID THOREAU'S "CIVIL DISOBEDI-
ence" (1849) and Martin Luther King, Jr.'s "Letter from Birmingham Jail" (1963) are the most famous documents in the American
tradition of nonviolence, without Adin Ballou's "Christian Non-
Resistance in All Its Important Bearings" (1846), would we have
the other two? In communities of education and action at least,
Adin Ballou's spirit is very much alive. Agape Community in
Ware, Massachusetts, resembles, in fact, Ballou's Hopedale Com-

munity, a 19th-century utopian experiment in nearby Milford. For both, the nonviolent gospel involving a refusal to kill and a commitment to social justice is central.

Reading Ballou's prose, one is struck by the apparent justice of his son-in-law's description of him as "a great power for good in the world, a noteworthy man of his age." For the tone and mood of Ballou's writings have a kind of sweet reasonableness about them, particularly when one remembers the difficulties he faced in espousing "Christian non-resistance" (nonviolence), a doctrine, as he put it, so "little understood, and almost everywhere spoken against."

Prior to Leo Tolstoy and Mohandas Gandhi, Adin Ballou contributed more to our understanding of nonviolence, perhaps, than anyone in recent history, and both the Russian count and the Indian mahatma studied Ballou's works and furthered the insights formulated in his carefully reasoned, generous spirited, and synthesizing treatment of the subject. Recognizing the controversial nature of his "unpopular doctrine" of nonviolence, Ballou proceeds with confidence and open-handedness to explore the full implications of his defense in "Christian Non-Resistance," believing it "as ancient as Christianity, and as true as the New Testament." For these reasons, characteristically, he asks that "friends and opposers be candid, just and generous" of his exposition, approving or condemning it "solely on its own intrinsic merits or demerits."

Born April 23, 1803, in Cumberland, Rhode Island, Adin Ballou was descended from the founders of that New England colony. At eighteen, he responded to what he regarded as a supernatural call to the ministry and subsequently headed Universalist societies in New York City and Milford, Massachusetts (where his statue stands today on the town common), and traveled throughout the Northeast as a popular preacher.

Ballou's writings in *Independent Messenger* (1831-1839) exercised considerable influence on Unitarian/Universalist thought, and his editing of pacifist and abolitionist journals, such as *The Nonresistant and Practical Christian* (1845-49), contributed to lively anarchist debates and the growth of Utopian communities in the decade just prior to the Civil War. Although Ballou regarded himself as "no antagonist to human government," his perspective challenged the basic ideologies of what we know now as state socialism or state capitalism. His position resembles Thoreau's, in "Civil Disobedience," written during the same period; for Ballou, government is "a mere cypher," with "no rightful claim to the allegiance of man."

In his remarks to a September 25, 1839, meeting of the Non-Resistance Society, in Boston, Ballou addressed the question whether we must "disobey parents, patriarchs, priests, kings, nobles, presidents, governors, generals, legislatures, constitutions, armies, mobs, *all* rather than disobey God?" His answer, resembling that of antiwar and anti-nuclear activists in recent decades, was, "We *must*; and then patiently endure the penal consequences."

In 1841, Ballou became co-founder and president of the Hopedale Community, on 250 acres of land near Milford. A utopian and Christian society based upon radical principles, it was an effort "to establish a state of society governed by divine moral principles, with as little as possible of mere human restraint." There, according to its constitution, "no individual shall suffer the evils of oppression, poverty, ignorance or vice through the influence or neglect of others."

In "What a Christian Non-Resistant Cannot Consistently Do," an opening section of *Christian Non-Resistance* (1846), Ballou listed seven commandmants that conscientious followers of Jesus should obey.

> He/she cannot kill, maim, or otherwise *absolutely injure* any human being, in personal self-defense, or for the sake of his family, or any thing he holds dear....He/she cannot be a member of any voluntary association, however orderly, respectable or allowable by law and general consent, *which declaratively* holds as *fundamental truth*, or claims as an essential right, or distinctly inculcates as sound doctrine, or approves as commendable in practice, *war, capital* punishment, or any other absolute personal injury.

Ballou stated, further, that the Christian Non-Resistant must not directly or indirectly "abet or encourage any act in others, nor demand, petition for, request, advise or approve the doing of any act, by an individual, association or government" that "would inflict, *threaten* to inflict, or *necessarily* cause to *be* inflicted *any absolute personal injury*." For the informing "sub-principle of Christian non-resistance," as Ballou argued first and Tolstoy later in *The Kingdom of God Is Within You* (1893) is "Evil can be overcome only with good." Anticipating Martin Luther King, Jr.'s counsel to civil rights activists and civil disobedients a century later, Ballou said *"Resist not personal injury with personal injury."* And in a verse concluding his introduction, Ballou describes Isaiah's vision, much in the manner of Edward Hick's well-known painting, "The Peaceable Kingdom":

The earth, so long a slaughter-field,
Shall yet an Eden bloom;
The *tiger* to the *lamb* shall yield,
And *War* descend the tomb:
For all shall feel the Saviour's love,
Reflected from the cross—
That love, that non-resistant love,
Which triumphed on the cross.

A vigorous debater, with a remarkable sense of the theoretical and practical implications of nonviolence, Ballou is at his best in addressing arguments justifying self-preservation. If self-preservation is the best method of protecting and preserving human life, Ballou asks, why have "fourteen thousand millions of human beings been slain by human means, in war and otherwise?" From such evidence, might one not conclude that such methods of self-preservation are "the off-spring of a purblind instinct—the cherished salvo of ignorance—the fatal charm of deluded credulity—the *supposed preserver*, but the *real destroyer* of the human family?

If only a few thousands, or even a few millions, had perished by the two-edged sword; ...[or] if the sword of self-defense had frightened the sword of aggression into its scabbard, there to consume in its rust; then might we admit that the common method of self-preservation was the true one. On the other hand, if everyone since the conflict of Cain and Abel had responded to robbery, murder, and killing with non-resistance, "would as many lives have been sacrificed, or as much real misery have been experienced by the human race," as has resulted from the usual method of responding to injury with injury?

As with so many of Ballou's arguments and questions, this reflection seems more timely, more pertinent to any discussion of "just war theory" today than it was a century ago.

But perhaps the most remarkable example of Adin Ballou's faithfulness to nonviolence was his steadfastness, as the other abolitionists and non-resisters came to justify the violent means of John Brown in his raid on Harper's Ferry in 1859 and of the national government's "war to end slavery" shortly afterward. One by one, Ballou's old friends and fellow non-resistants drifted away, forgot their earlier commitment to nonviolence—William Lloyd Garrison, Thomas Wentworth Higginson, even that most persistent nonviolent activist, Stephen Symonds Foster.

In his autobiography, Ballou set their earlier statements beside their later justifications of war. Almost alone among his old radical friends, he continued to insist on just means for just ends, carefully thinking through as well what his grandson's response to the wartime draft should be, as a non-resistant. In the last years of his remarkable active life as writer, lecturer, and clergyman, he devoted himself to writing his family and commuunity history, but in general never repudiated or turned away from the values and principles associated with resistance to violence and discrimination that had informed his life and writings since he first formulated them fifty years before.

BY ADIN BALLOU

Autobiography of Adin Ballou, 1803-1890, Containing an Elaborate Record and Narrative of His Life From Infancy to Old Age, with Appendixes. William S. Heywood, ed. Philadelphia: Porcupine Press, (1896) 1975.

Christian Non-Resistance, in All Its Important Bearings, Illustrated and Defended. Philadelphia: J. Miller M'Kim, 1846.

History of the Hopedale Community, From Its Inception to Its Virtual Submergence in the Hopedale Parish. William S. Heywood, ed. Lowell, Mass.: Thompson & Hill, 1897.

Practical Christian Socialism: A Conversational Exposition of the True System of Human Society. New York: Fowlers and Wells, 1854.

ABOUT ADIN BALLOU

Patterns of Anarchy: A Collection of Writings on the Anarchist Tradition. Leonard I. Krimerman and Lewis Perry, eds. New York: Anchor Book, 1966.

Society of Friends (Quakers), Mennonites, Church of the Brethren

IN THE PAST, THEY EVOKED FURY, EVEN HATRED, FROM conventional Christians who were perplexed by the refusal of Quakers, Mennonites, and Brethren to take up arms against their "enemies." Today, members of the three historic peace churches are regarded as experienced, even inspiring peacemakers.

Through personal suffering in the face of community indifference or hostility, they set the pattern for conscientious objection to war and to other practices that undermined their religious commitment to peace. Thousands of Quakers, Mennonites, and Brethren suffered death and imprisonment, in this country and abroad, for conscientiously refusing to kill their brothers and sisters, whatever the justification given by the State.

How many Americans know the heavy price paid by members of the historic peace churches in helping to guarantee our free exercise of religion? In the Massachusetts Bay Colony, for example, Quakers were automatically imprisoned on their arrival in the colonies; and four of them, including Mary Dyer—whose statue overlooks the Boston Common—were hanged for returning to Boston to worship as they pleased. In the same period, a young servant girl and a middle-aged mother of five children, after being transferred from shipboard to prison, were stripped naked, searched for witchcraft, and held for five weeks in darkness.

Quakers persisted, nonetheless, showing immense courage in upholding their rights as citizens. While William Leddra was being considered for the death penalty, Wenlock Christison, who had already been banished on pain of death, calmly walked into the courtroom. And while he was being tried, Edward Wharton, ordered earlier to leave the colony or lose his life, wrote of his decision to remain to the authorities.

In 17th-century Virginia as well, Quakers were regarded as "unreasonable and turbulent...teaching and publishing lies, miracles, false visions, prophecies and doctrines." In the 18th century, Thomas Paine ridiculed Quakers who refused to take up arms in the revolutionary struggle against the English; and in the 19th century, Nathaniel Hawthorne, that most principled of storytellers, characterized Quakers as troublemakers threatening to rend the delicate social fabric of the new nation.

Among the Mennonites, resolutions adopted by a 1961 General Conference in Pennsylvania echo their theology and the statements by other peace churches since 1725:

1. Our love and ministry must go out to all, whether friend or foe.
2. While rejecting any ideology which...seeks to destroy the Christian faith, we cannot take any attitude or commit any act contrary to Christian love....

3. If our country becomes involved in war, we shall...avoid joining in any wartime hysteria of hatred, revenge, and retaliation.

Together with this refusal to kill went a commitment to "justice for all." The Mennonites, for example, were among the first to resist slavery in the U.S.; one account describes an 18th-century Mennonite who slept in the forest rather than accept hospitality from a slaveholder.

Although relatively small in comparision with other religious groups—the Quakers, for example, the largest of the three memberships, number only 120,000 in the U.S.—the peace churches have exercised an influence on American political traditions out of all proportion to their numbers. Famous libertarians who grew up in Quaker households include Thomas Paine, John Woolman, John Greenleaf Whittier, Lucretia Mott, Walt Whitman, and Susan B. Anthony.

Whatever liberties Americans enjoy relating to freedom of assembly and the press and the principle of conscientious objection have their beginnings in the witness and persistence of the historic peace communities. The principle of conscientious objection alone, first recognized in Rhode Island and, in 1940, under Selective Service laws and regulations initiated at that time, owes much to the peace churches and to related organizations initiated at the time of the First World War.

The Society of Friends (Quakers) dates from 1652, when George Fox (1624-91) gathered a group of Seekers and other Children of Light around him in England. Although not all those Quakers were pacifists, within eight years, at the time of the Restoration of Charles II, they declared to the King:

We utterly deny all outward wars and strife and fighting with outward weapons, for any end or under any pretence whatsoever, and we do certainly know, and so testify to the world that the spirit of Christ, which leads us into all Truth, will never move us to fight and war against any man with outward weapons, neither for the kingdom of Christ, nor for the kingdoms of this world.

Later in the 17th century, William Penn (1644-1718), another Englishman jailed for his pacifist beliefs, founded a large and influential Quaker community in the American colonies. In 1681, before coming to the colonies, he summarized the general philosophy of the peace churches in a letter to Native Americans, saying that God "made the world and all things therein...not to devour and destroy one another, but [to] live soberly and kindly together in the world." He generally agreed with his contemporary, Edward Burroughs, who thought that Quakers "must obey God only and deny active obedience for conscience's sake, and patiently suffer what is inflicted upon us for our disobedience of men."

William Penn's hope for the New World, his vision, was based upon a famous passage from the Book of Isaiah, whereby the lion and the lamb would lie together, and all of nature would live in harmony. Edward Hicks, an 18th century Quaker painter—and later artists such as Fritz Eichenberg (1901-90)—popularized that image on canvas, in woodcuts and lithographs, in many versions of "The Peaceable Kingdom."

Understanding how that vision might be lived out has been a three-century effort of trial and error, action and meditation, commitment and hesitation by these small communities of believers. How and when, in conscience, must one "stick up for God," as Ammon Hennacy used to say, and when may one "render unto Caesar"? While Christian churches justified "killing for Christ," with arguments formulated by apologists such as Augustine and other "just war" theorists, Quakers, Mennonites, and Brethren, in association with other pacifists, nonviolent resisters, and Christian anarchists, have endured continual hardship in working to eradicate injustices perpetrated by war and violence.

At the time of the First World War, for example, as a way not only to resist war, but also to demonstrate "a service of love," the Society of Friends in the U.S., with encouragement from English Friends, initiated a service arm of the Society, the American Friends Service Committee. That organization, which maintains regional offices throughout the country, has trained thousands of people for work among refugees around the world and for nonviolent campaigns at home—for civil rights and nuclear disarmament, as well as against the Vietnam war and arms shipments to Central America.

The Mennonites, named for Menno Simons (1496-1561), and the Church of the Brethren both trace their origins to 16th-century Anabaptists, who resisted any union between church and state. Originating in Germany and Switzerland respectively, they believed in freedom of conscience and condemned religious persecution of any kind. The writings of Christopher Sauer, a radical pietist and uncompromising pacifist, influenced both groups in early Pennsylvania, where they joined with their Quaker neighbors in supporting a beneficent government. Sauer, who spoke of soldiers as "military slaves," said that true followers of Jesus could not kill and that participation in war was contrary to the gospel.

At the time of the American Revolution, Mennonites, Brethren, and Quakers composed a significant percentage of the population in the colonies, with the latter group numbering about 50,000 among a total population of 1.6 million. They were responsible for establishing friendly relationships with Native Americans, and later, for making Pennsylvania the first state to abolish slavery. In the 19th century, they provided much of the leadership for the abolitionist movement.

Among the peace churches, their colleges, service committees, and publishing houses are especially important in maintaining and expanding their influence in the wider community. For the Quakers, they include Swarthmore College and Haverford College, in Pennsylvania, and Earlham College, in Indiana; the main office, in Philadelphia, of the American Friends Service Committee, which received the Nobel Prize for Peace in 1947; and the office of Friends Committee on National Legislation, in Washington, D.C. For the Mennonites, they include Goshen College, in Indiana, and Bethel College, in Kansas; and for the Church of the Brethren, McPherson College, in Kansas, and Manchester College, in Indiana. Many peace and justice organizations that eventually became independent of these churches also owe much to their inspiration and guidance, and the larger Christian denominations particularly, have much to learn from the religious education programs and publications sponsored by the peace churches on moral issues relating to justice and peace. The following statement by a prominent member of the Brethren about 18th-century Lutherans, Calvinists, and Catholics remains true today: "What is still more horrible, they go publicly to war, and slaughter one another by the thousands."

In rejecting war, even in revolutionary struggle, the peace churches run risks today similar to those they ran three centuries ago, when they were imprisoned and beaten, their homes seized or burned for their refusal to take up arms against the British. Recognizing "that of God in every person" and "proceeding as the way opens," Quakers choose nonviolence, not because it guarantees results, but because they must, as Margaret Hope Bacon has said. Along that way lies suffering, even death, but only through peaceful means, they argue, does anyone achieve a peaceful end. And even for many who cannot accept the discipline of that life, the historic peace churches—by their witness and experience—remain central to any sustained effort "to construct peace." In their sustained effort to build "the peaceable kingdom" by resolving conflict and initiating social change without killing, they claim particular authority in building nonviolent alternatives to the violence of the status quo.

ABOUT SOCIETY OF FRIENDS (QUAKERS), MENNONITES, CHURCH OF THE BRETHREN

Bacon, Margaret Hope. *The Quiet Rebels: The Story of the Quakers in America*. Philadelphia: New Society Publishers, 1985.

Brock, Peter. *Pacifism in the U.S. from the Colonial Era to the First World War*. Princeton, N.J.: Princeton University Press, 1968.

Brown, Dale W. *Brethren and Pacifism*. Elgin, Ill.: Brethren Press, 1970.

Keim, Albert N, and Grant M. Stoltzfus. *The Politics of Conscience: The Historic Peace Churches and America at War, 1917-1955*. Scottdale, Penn.: Herald Press, 1988.

Yoder, John H. *What Would You Do?: A Serious Answer to a Standard Question*. Scottdale, Penn.: Herald Press, 1983.

SEATTLE
1786?-1866

IN SPITE OF THEIR RICH TRADITION OF NONVIOLENCE
since the 17th century, Americans give little attention to those
who made peace, not war, or those who resisted slavery and injustice without killing. Seldom doing justice to our apostles of
nonviolence, we find it even harder to build on the contributions
of those who lived on this land twenty, thirty, maybe 40,000 years
before white settlers arrived: the Native Americans who named
the rivers and settlements and resisted humiliation and discrimination—even as they were forced to surrender their homeland.

In a history or "geography" of nonviolence, certain Native American tribes and leaders deserve a significant place. (Ammon Hennacy, 1893-1970, Christian anarchist, regarded the Hopi as particularly noteworthy.) Although Native Americans were not usually pacifists, they often went to great lengths to live peacefully, honorably among invaders; many of them avoided, as long as they could, confrontations that endangered their own or others' enjoyment of the rich, beautiful, and productive region of the earth they shared.

Increasingly, as human beings come to understand the communality of their fate and their interdependence with nature, they acknowledge the contributions of each culture to this understanding. Books and materials in the U.S. emphasizing the necessity of good stewardship of the "sacred" earth almost inevitably quote a saying, poem, or prayer by a Native American; the following lines from a poem by Tahirussawichi, a Pawnee priest (Kurahus), are representative.

All things move with the breath of the new day;
Everywhere life is renewed.

This is very mysterious;
We are speaking of something very sacred,
Although it happens every day.

Such reverence for the earth reflects a vivid sense of the simplicity and mystery of life, which Mohandas Gandhi and others have regarded as the spiritual bases of nonviolence. (Other Indian writings describe our endangering our own and nature's survival by careless, "modern" habits.)

Because of his nonviolent ethic, it seems appropriate to conclude this selection of portraits by focusing on the life of Chief Seattle, the eloquent, peaceable leader in the Pacific Northwest. What little we know of him suggests his commitment to the best values of Native American culture and of Christianity, following his conversion in 1830.

Born near Puget Sound about 1786, Seattle (also Seathl or Sealth) was the descendant of chiefs of the Suquamish and

Dwamish tribes, and was himself subsequently chief of the Dwamish, Suquamish, and allied Indian tribes. Shortly before he was born, sea expeditions looking for the mythical Northwest Passage brought Mexican, English, and Russian expeditions to his area. This led to profit-making schemes, which involved the killing of various animals, including sea otters, for furs. When most of the otters were gone, foreign explorers discontinued their raids for awhile. Then, in the early 19th century, overland expeditions brought Lewis and Clark and others to the region.

In an effort to declare its hold on the territory, the U.S. Congress—and later the Monroe Doctrine—disputed the claims of other countries in the Pacific Northwest. In their deliberations, of course, neither Congress nor foreign nations consulted Native American residents about rights and privileges.

Initially, Seattle—like his father and other Native Americans before him—was friendly and helpful to settlers in the region. Gradually, however, he had to contend with increasing encroachments and claims to the land. Throughout, he demonstrated his commitment to "making peace" in the way he dealt with new residents and with neighboring tribes.

In 1844, James Polk was elected president of the U.S., partly on the strength of his promise to settle boundary disputes with the English, to the North. At mid-century, after the Gold Rush and what detractors called President Polk's "trumped-up war with Mexico," white settlers moved up from California in larger numbers to Oregon and Washington, eventually giving Chief Seattle's name to a settlement on Puget Sound.

In 1853, after Washington was named a U.S. territory, Governor Isaac Ingalls Stevens pushed through treaties with Native Americans at hurried councils; Indians later claimed, probably accurately, that their signatures had been forged or the conditions of settlement inadequately explained. The governor had refused to translate the documents into native languages, using instead Chinook, "a kind of *lingua franca* made up of words from a variety of Indian languages, with French and English." At one of these deliberations, a Native American spokesman responded by describing the psychological effect of such unjust seizures of his land:

How is it I have been troubled in mind? If your mothers were here in this country who gave you birth, and suckled you, and while you were suckling some person came and took away your mother and left you alone and sold your mother, how would you feel then? This is our mother, this country, as if we drew our living from her.

When President Franklin Pierce wanted to buy more land from Chief Seattle and his tribe, Seattle reluctantly agreed in the hope of avoiding war.

Later, when Governor Stevens addressed settlers and Indians at an important gathering, Seattle made an extended reply. He warned against misuse of the region's land, air, and water in his address, which environmentalists have quoted and distributed frequently in recent years.

His justly famous speech begins with an acknowlegement of the spirit of place, informed by deceased ancestors but soon to harbor others: "Yonder sky that has wept tears of compassion upon my people for centuries untold, and which to us appears changeless and eternal, may change." In a wry, rather satiric vein, Seattle admits his people's powerlessness before the governor's leader in far-away Washington, D.C., and the upheaval that Native Americans must endure:

> The White Chief says that Big Chief at Washington sends us greetings of friendship and goodwill. This is kind of him for we know he has little need of our friendship in return.

Refusing to mourn his people's decay or to reproach "our paleface brothers with hastening it," Seattle dwells instead on the collective future that old and new residents share, suggesting that the tragedy of his people was not theirs alone.

In a powerful, almost prophetic conclusion, Seattle describes the conflicting values in the culture then overpowering his own. His understanding of those conflicts foreshadows, in some ways, the dilemma of nonviolent activists trying to mediate among similar conflicting values a century-and-a-half later.

> To us the ashes of our ancesters are sacred and their resting

place is hallowed ground. You wander far from the graves of your ancestors and seemingly without regret....

Your dead cease to love you and the land of their nativity as soon as they pass the portals of the tomb and wander beyond the stars; they are soon forgotten and never return. Our dead never forget the beautiful world that gave them being....

Reconciling this conflict between the living and the dead, Seattle seems to say, might eliminate ecological disasters he sees in the future:

Humankind did not weave the web of life. We are but one strand within it. Whatever we do to the web, we do to ourselves....Continue to soil your bed, and you will one night suffocate in your own waste.

In theme, Seattle's speech resembles the theme of Muriel Rukeyser's poem quoted in this book's introduction and title, "To construct peace... to reconcile/ Waking with sleeping, ourselves with each other,/ Ourselves with ourselves." For the dead, "the sleeping," continue to influence the world after they are gone, Seattle says; even as the last Red Man perishes, his memory will become "a myth among the white man," whose shores will swarm with the invisible members of the tribe:

At night when the streets of your cities and villages are silent and you think them deserted, they will throng with the returning hosts that once filled them and still love this beautiful land.

Recognizing that armed conflict with U.S. military forces meant probable extinction of his small band, Seattle was among the first signers of the Port Elliott Treaty of 1855, which established a reservation for various Native American tribes in that region.

Chief Seattle died on June 7, 1866, on the Port Madison Reservation and is buried in the Suquamish cemetery near the city bearing his name.

BY SEATTLE

Chronicles of American Indian Protest. Council on Interracial Books for Children, ed. Greenwich, Conn.: Fawcett Publications, 1971.

Indian Oratory: Famous Speeches by Noted Indian Chieftans. V. C. Vanderwerth, ed. Norman: University of Oklahoma Press, 1971, 117-22.

"Chief Seattle's Message," *The Power of the People: Active Nonviolence in the United States.* Robert Cooney and Helen Michalowski, eds. Philadelphia: New Society Publishers, 1987.

ABOUT SEATTLE

Dockstader, Frederick J. *Great North American Indians: Profiles in Life and Leadership.* New York: Van Nostrand Reinhold Co., 1977.

Hughes, J. Donald. *American Indian Ecology.* El Paso: Texas Western Press, 1983.

Other Justice and Peace titles from Twenty-Third Publications...

Proclaiming Justice & Peace
Papal Documents from Rerum Novarum
through Centesimus Annus
Edited by Michael Walsh and Brian Davies
100 years of Catholic social teaching, represented by 14 documents
that respond to a panorama of human needs, anxieties and concerns.
Editors' commentaries situate the statements in historical context.
ISBN: 0-89622-481-3, 522 pages, 6" X 9", Cloth, $29.95 (order B-54)

Whispers of Revelation: Discovering the Spirit of the Poor
Bill and Patty Coleman
Personal experiences of the authors living among the poor in Mexico,
as they probe for the implications to us today of the Gospel stories
about poverty and the poor.
ISBN: 0-89622-505-4, 208 pages, 5 1/2" X 8 1/2", Paper, $9.95 (order B-60)

Active Nonviolence: A Way of Personal Peace
Gerard A. Vanderhaar
Offers practical advice on how to live a creative, fulfilling and
peaceful life.
ISNB: 0-89622-392-2, 144 pages, 5 1/2" X 8 1/2", Paper, $7.95 (order C-15)

Profiles in Liberation: 36 Portraits of Third World Theologians
Deane William Ferm
36 Portraits of Third World theologians that highlight their
contributions to religious thought and practice.
ISBN: 0-89622-377-9, 217 pages, 5 1/2" X 8 1/2", Paper, $9.95 (order W-73)

Available at religious bookstores or from
TWENTY-THIRD PUBLICATIONS
P.O. Box 180 • Mystic, CT 06355 • 1-800-321-0411